OXFORD
UNIVERSITY PRESS

Great Clarendon Street, Oxford OX2 6DP

Oxford University Press is a department of the University of Oxford.
It furthers the University's objective of excellence in research, scholarship,
and education by publishing worldwide in

Oxford   New York

Auckland   Cape Town   Dar es Salaam   Hong Kong   Karachi
Kuala Lumpur   Madrid   Melbourne   Mexico City   Nairobi
New Delhi   Shanghai   Taipei   Toronto

With offices in

Argentina   Austria   Brazil   Chile   Czech Republic   France   Greece
Guatemala   Hungary   Italy   Japan   South Korea   Poland   Portugal
Singapore   Switzerland   Thailand   Turkey   Ukraine   Vietnam

Oxford is a registered trade mark of Oxford University Press
in the UK and in certain other countries

Text reproduced courtesy of Oxford World's Classics

Text © Oxford University Press 2008
Explanatory Notes © Richard Gill 2007

British Library Cataloguing in Publication Data
Data available

ISBN: 978-019-838689 6
10 9 8 7 6 5 4 3

Typeset in India by TNQ

Printed in Great Britain by CPI Antony Rowe, Chippenham

Paper used in the production of this book is a natural, recyclable product made
from wood grown in sustainable forests. The manufacturing process conforms
to the environmental regulations of the country of origin.

Contents

Introduction: English Literature

Unit F663 is the examined unit for English Literature A2, and carries 60% of the marks at A2. This text has been prescribed for Section B of the examination, where you are required to explore connections and comparisons between a drama text and a poetry text. In this introduction, you will find advice to help you prepare for the examination and the ways in which your work will be assessed.

Choice of texts

For Section B study, there is a choice of four drama texts and four poetry texts; your teacher will select one text from each group of four. There is a free choice of pairings of texts, and your teacher will look for connections between the texts he or she chooses. For example, there may be similarities of tone (e.g. humorous or heroic) or of subject matter (e.g. religious faith or the treatment of women). When you are preparing for the examination, it will be important to ensure that you know the individual texts in detail, and also that you have considered very thoroughly the possible connections and comparisons between them.

How to approach the examination

There will be a choice of six questions of which you can choose any one, regardless of your choice of set texts. These questions will ask about a central idea (e.g. power, or tragedy, or the role of women), and ask you to compare the treatment of this idea in your chosen texts.

For example, an essay question might read:

> By comparing one poetry and one drama text you have studied, discuss ways in which writers explore the dangers and delights of ambition.

The question begins by asking for comparison. You should understand this as an invitation to look for any similarities or differences, or any other connections between the two texts which help you to answer the question (see AO3 below). Most questions will ask you to look at 'ways in which' the writer treats the area under discussion; this part of the question directs you to consider the variety of approaches and methods used by writers in their treatment of the central theme or idea (see AO2 below). It is important to look carefully at the way the question is worded: in the question currently under discussion, for example, you are not just invited to discuss the theme of 'ambition' – you are asked to consider 'the <u>dangers and delights</u> of ambition'. To receive high marks, therefore, you need to consider carefully and explicitly both the destabilising and the rewarding qualities of ambition in your answer.

In an English Literature examination, there is never just one correct way to answer the question; however, there are some useful techniques which may help you to maximise your marks. It is helpful to write a short introduction to your essay which addresses the central idea in the question and relates it briefly to the texts you have chosen. The main body of your essay should include detailed discussion of the central idea, relating it to both of your set texts. You should ensure that you give the two texts roughly equal space in your answer, and that you include passages of sustained comparison: answers which deal with the two texts separately – perhaps with some perfunctory comparison by way of conclusion – will limit the marks they can achieve for looking at 'connections and comparisons' (see AO3 below). Finally, you should consider writing a conclusion which expresses succinctly the most important similarities and/or differences between your two texts in relation to the central idea in the question.

You should aim to use quotations to support your answer, especially with reference to AO2 (see below). Remember that AO2 can also be satisfied by more general references to the text, however, so that your own brief account of an event or moment in the text will sometimes be as helpful as a quotation.

What are the Assessment Objectives?

Your examiner will mark your work on the basis of four

Assessment Objectives (AO1, AO2, AO3 and AO4); the marking will be weighted in favour of AO3 and AO4.

Assessment Objective 1

> Articulate **creative**, **informed** and **relevant** responses to literary texts, using **appropriate terminology and concepts**, and **coherent, accurate written expression**.

Answers should be **creative** in the sense that good candidates will respond imaginatively, selecting and combining interesting and telling moments from the poetry and drama texts which help to arrive at an answer to the question.

They should be **informed** by a reasonable level of awareness concerning the set texts; for example, of information about the writers, the nature of poems or plays of the period in question and of poetry and drama in general. Such information should support the answer but not be allowed to dominate it.

Above all, answers should be **relevant**: when writing practice essays, it can be helpful to check every sentence to ensure that it is helping to form an answer to the question. You should aim to use key terms from the question at times during your essay, and especially in the conclusion.

During your study of your set texts, you should become familiar with **appropriate terminology and concepts**: for example, you should be able to discuss ideas such as 'dramatic irony' and 'metaphor'.

Coherent, accurate written expression is an essential part of a good answer: you should check the accuracy of your spelling and punctuation and especially your grammar to ensure that your essay is completed to a high standard and can be readily understood.

Assessment Objective 2

> Demonstrate **detailed critical understanding** in **analysing** the ways in which **structure, form and language** shape meanings in literary texts.

This Assessment Objective requires you to look closely at the detail of your set texts. You need to show how the writer of your poem or play achieves his or her effects through choices of language, form and structure. Methods of writing will vary according to the text you are studying: comments on **language** might include references to allusion (e.g. Pope's use of classical reference in *The Rape of the Lock*) or dialogue (e.g. polite conversation in *The School for Scandal*). Writing about **form** might lead you to consider choices the writer has made within his or her chosen genre (aspects of the revenge tragedy in *The Duchess of Malfi*, for example, or the use of the sonnet form in John Donne). Material relating to **structure** might focus on a writer's use of contrasting passages (e.g. scenes in *Dr Faustus* dealing with Faustus's enjoyments and those with his damnation, or Milton's use of narrative and dialogue in *Paradise Lost*). Remember, it is not enough to list methods used by a writer, even if you offer examples; you must always analyse the effects of the writing as well.

Assessment Objective 3

> **Explore connections and comparisons between different literary texts**, informed by interpretations of other readers.

This Assessment Objective combines different ideas, and here the main requirement is that you should **explore connections and comparisons** between your poetry and drama texts. During your answer, you should ensure that you offer some detailed and sustained comparison to show how the poet and the playwright you have studied compare in their treatment of the theme or idea in the question. You might find differences or similarities in the attitudes revealed in the text, or in the techniques used to express ideas (if you compare techniques, you will find that you are responding to AO2 and AO3 at the same time). You will find it helpful to bear in mind important features of the genre in which each text has been written. You can also receive credit for evidence that your answer is informed by **interpretations of other readers**, but this aspect of AO3 is of secondary importance in this section of the paper.

Assessment Objective 4

> Demonstrate understanding of the significance and influence of the **contexts** in which literary texts are written and received.

This Assessment Objective requires you to think about ideas and information in addition to the set texts. These ideas might be social or historical (e.g. what was the role of women in society at the time your text is written or is set?); they could be literary (what is this text like in relation to others by the same writer, or by his or her contemporaries?); they could be biographical (what were the important influences on the life of the writer when he or she produced this work?). It is also helpful to consider different critical reactions to the text over the period of time since its publication – or, in the case of drama, the performance history of your chosen play. In this part of the exam, it will be especially helpful to consider your set texts in the context of the genre in which they were written (see 'Cross-genre Comparison' below). Contextual study requires some research and learning, but should never be allowed to dominate an answer; take care to avoid writing long paragraphs of contextual information which do not support your argument.

Cross-genre Comparison

One of the most demanding aspects of this section is the requirement for 'cross-genre comparison'. At AS level, you will have covered techniques for comparison of two texts in Task 2 of your coursework unit; however, these texts may well have been from the same genre, so that you were comparing like with like. In Section B of F663, as in your A2 coursework, you are required to compare texts from different genres: here, poetry and drama, and, in your coursework, poetry and prose. For this reason, you will find it especially helpful to investigate and discuss characteristics of the genres of your chosen texts, and to use this study as part of the basis for your comparison. You might wish to ask yourself some of the following questions about the texts you are studying:

- What are the chief characteristics of drama? (Think about characters, action, dialogue, conflict, the role of the audience, etc.)
- What are the chief characteristics of poetry? (Think about form, imagery, concentration of linguistic effect, etc.)
- How 'poetic' is my drama text? (Is it written completely or partly in verse? Does the writer make significant use of poetic techniques such as elaborate similes or couplets?)
- How 'dramatic' is my poetry text? (Does it have a narrative line? Characters? A strong speaking voice? Does it include passages which deal with action or conflict? Does it lend itself to performance?)
- Why might a poet and a dramatist treat an idea or a theme in a different way? What are the constraints and opportunities offered by these different genres?

If you can supply detailed answers to these questions, preferably with textual support (detailed references or quotations), you will have completed some very effective preparation for this part of the exam. You may also like to use an appropriately adapted version of these questions to support your A2 coursework preparation; it certainly makes sense to be aware of the similarities of these two tasks, so that you can transfer the skills you learn between them.

OCR Specification Excerpt

The OCR GCE specification for English Literature is the document on which assessment is based; it specifies the content and skills to be covered in delivering a course of study. At all times, therefore, these excerpts should be read in conjunction with the specification. If clarification on a particular point is needed then reference should be in the first instance to the specification.

Unit Content

A2 Unit F663: *Drama and Poetry pre-1800* (Closed text)

There are two sections to this unit:

• Section A: Shakespeare
• *Section B: Drama and Poetry pre-1800*

Section B: Drama and Poetry pre-1800

This section requires candidates to explore contrasts, connections and comparisons between different literary texts. In their answers candidates must refer to **one drama text** and **one poetry text** from the lists of texts set for this section.

There will be a choice of six different questions each with a different focus. Candidates must select **one** question, and base their answer on a comparative study, with substantial discussion of both texts.

Candidates are required to show critical understanding in analysing ways in which structure, form and language shape meaning and demonstrate understanding of the significance and influence of the contexts in which literary texts are written and understood.

Advanced GCE Scheme of Assessment

A2 Unit F663: Drama and Poetry pre-1800

30% of the total Advanced GCE marks
2 h written paper 60 marks

Section B: Drama and Poetry pre-1800

Candidates are required to write an essay that is a comparative study of one drama and one poetry text.

Candidates are assessed on:

AO1: articulate creative, informed and relevant responses to literary texts, using appropriate terminology and concepts, and coherent, accurate written expression;

AO2: demonstrate detailed critical understanding in analysing the ways in which structure, form and language shape meanings in literary texts;

AO3: explore connections and comparisons between different literary texts, informed by interpretations of other readers;

AO4: demonstrate understanding of the significance and influence of the contexts in which literary texts are written and received.

Assessment Criteria for A2 Unit F663: *Drama and Poetry pre-1800*

Band 6 **26–30** **marks**	AO 1	• excellent and consistently detailed understanding of texts and question; • consistently fluent, precise writing in appropriate register; • critical terminology used accurately and consistently; • well-structured, coherent and detailed argument consistently developed.
	AO 2	• well-developed and consistently detailed discussion of effects (including dramatic effects) of language, form and structure; • excellent and consistently effective use of analytical methods; • consistently effective use of quotations and references to text, critically addressed, blended into discussion.
	AO 3	• excellent and consistently detailed comparative analysis of relationships between texts; • well-informed and effective exploration of different readings of text.
	AO 4	• consistently well-developed and consistently detailed understanding of the significance and influence of contexts in which literary texts are written and understood, as appropriate to the question.
Band 5 **21–25** **marks**	AO 1	• good and secure understanding of texts and question; • good level of coherence and accuracy in writing, in appropriate register; • critical terminology used accurately; • well-structured argument with clear line of development.
	AO 2	• developed and good level of detail in discussion of effects (including dramatic effects) of language, form and structure; • good use of analytical methods; • good use of quotations and references to text, generally critically addressed.
	AO 3	• good, clear comparative analysis of relationships between texts; • judgements informed by recognition of different readings of texts.
	AO 4	• good, clear evaluation of the significance and influence of contexts in which literary texts are written and understood, as appropriate to the question.

Band 4 **16–20** **marks**	AO 1	• competent understanding of texts and question; • clear writing in generally appropriate register; • critical terminology used appropriately; • straightforward arguments generally competently structured.
	AO 2	• generally developed discussion of effects (including dramatic effects) of language, form and structure; • competent use of analytical methods; • competent use of illustrative quotations and references to support discussion.
	AO 3	• competent comparative discussion of relationships between texts; • answer informed by some reference to different readings of texts.
	AO 4	• competent understanding of the significance and influence of contexts in which literary texts are written and understood, as appropriate to the question.
Band 3 **11–15** **marks**	AO 1	• some understanding of texts and main elements of question; • some clear writing, some inconsistencies in register; • some appropriate use of critical terminology; • some structured argument evident, lacking development and/or full illustration.
	AO 2	• some attempt to develop discussion of effects (including dramatic effects) of language, form and structure; • some attempt at using analytical methods; • some use of quotations/references as illustration.
	AO 3	• some attempt to develop comparative discussion of relationships between texts; • some awareness of different readings of texts.
	AO 4	• some understanding of the significance and influence of contexts in which literary texts are written and understood, as appropriate to the question.

Band 2 **6–10** **marks**	AO 1	• limited understanding of texts and partial attempt at question; • inconsistent writing, frequent instances of technical error, limited use of appropriate register; • limited use of critical terminology; • limited attempt to structure discussion; tendency to lose track of argument.
	AO 2	• limited discussion of effects (including dramatic effects) of language, form and structure; • descriptive or narrative comment; limited use of analytical methods; • limited or inconsistent use of quotations, uncritically presented.
	AO 3	• limited comparative discussion of relationships between texts; • limited awareness of different readings of texts.
	AO 4	• limited understanding of the significance and influence of contexts in which literary texts are written and understood, as appropriate to the question.
Band 1 **0–5** **marks**	AO 1	• very little or no relevant understanding of texts; • very inconsistent writing with persistent serious technical errors, very little or no use of appropriate register; • persistently inaccurate or no use of critical terminology; • undeveloped, very fragmentary discussion.
	AO 2	• very little relevant or no discussion of effects (including dramatic effects) of language, form and structure; • very infrequent commentary; very little or no use of analytical methods; • very few quotations (eg one or two) used (and likely to be incorrect), or no quotations used.
	AO 3	• very little or no relevant comparative discussion of relationships between texts; • very little or no relevant awareness of different readings of texts.
	AO 4	• very little reference to (and likely to be irrelevant) or no understanding of the significance and influence of contexts in which literary texts are written and understood, as appropriate to the question.

John Donne

Selected Poems

Songs and Sonnets

Air and Angels

Twice or thrice had I loved thee,
Before I knew thy face or name;
So in a voice, so in a shapeless flame,
Angels affect us oft, and worshipped be;
5   Still when, to where thou wert, I came,
Some lovely glorious nothing I did see,
    But since my soul, whose child love is,
Takes limbs of flesh, and else could nothing do,
    More subtle than the parent is
10 Love must not be, but take a body too,
    And therefore what thou wert, and who
      I bid love ask, and now
That it assume thy body, I allow,
And fix itself in thy lip, eye, and brow.

15 Whilst thus to ballast love, I thought,
And so more steadily to have gone,
With wares which would sink admiration,
I saw, I had love's pinnace overfraught,
    Every thy hair for love to work upon
20 Is much too much, some fitter must be sought;
    For, nor in nothing, nor in things
Extreme, and scatt'ring bright, can love inhere;
    Then as an angel, face and wings
Of air, not pure as it, yet pure doth wear,
25   So thy love may be my love's sphere;
      Just such disparity
As is 'twixt air and angels' purity,
'Twixt women's love, and men's will ever be.

The Anniversary

All kings, and all their favourites,
    All glory of honours, beauties, wits,
The sun itself, which makes times, as they pass,
Is elder by a year, now, than it was
5   When thou and I first one another saw:
All other things, to their destruction draw,
    Only our love hath no decay;
This, no tomorrow hath, nor yesterday,
Running it never runs from us away,
10   But truly keeps his first, last, everlasting day.

Two graves must hide thine and my corse,
    If one might, death were no divorce,
Alas, as well as other princes, we,
(Who prince enough in one another be,)
15   Must leave at last in death, these eyes, and ears,
Oft fed with true oaths, and with sweet salt tears;
    But souls where nothing dwells but love
(All other thoughts being inmates) then shall prove
This, or a love increased there above,
20   When bodies to their graves, souls from their graves
    remove.

And then we shall be throughly blessed,
    But we no more, than all the rest.
Here upon earth, we are kings, and none but we
Can be such kings, nor of such subjects be;
25   Who is so safe as we? where none can do
Treason to us, except one of us two.
    True and false fears let us refrain,
Let us love nobly, and live, and add again
Years and years unto years, till we attain
30   To write threescore, this is the second of our reign.

The Apparition

When by thy scorn, O murderess, I am dead,
And that thou think'st thee free
From all solicitation from me,
Then shall my ghost come to thy bed,
5   And thee, feigned vestal, in worse arms shall see;
Then thy sick taper will begin to wink,
And he, whose thou art then, being tired before,
Will, if thou stir, or pinch to wake him, think
    Thou call'st for more,
10   And in false sleep will from thee shrink,
And then poor aspen wretch, neglected thou
Bathed in a cold quicksilver sweat wilt lie
    A verier ghost than I;
What I will say, I will not tell thee now,
15   Lest that preserve thee; and since my love is spent,
I had rather thou shouldst painfully repent,
Than by my threatenings rest still innocent.

Break of Day

'Tis true, 'tis day, what though it be?
O wilt thou therefore rise from me?
Why should we rise, because 'tis light?
Did we lie down, because 'twas night?
5   Love which in spite of darkness brought us hither,
Should in despite of light keep us together.

Light hath no tongue, but is all eye;
If it could speak as well as spy,
This were the worst, that it could say,
10   That being well, I fain would stay,
And that I loved my heart and honour so,
That I would not from him, that had them, go.

Must business thee from hence remove?
Oh, that's the worst disease of love,
15   The poor, the foul, the false, love can
Admit but not the busied man.
He which hath business, and makes love, doth do
Such wrong, as when a married man doth woo.

The Canonization

For God's sake hold your tongue, and let me love,
　　Or chide my palsy, or my gout,
My five grey hairs, or ruined fortune flout,
　　With wealth your state, your mind with arts
　　　improve,
5　　　Take you a course, get you a place,
　　　Observe his Honour, or his Grace,
Or the King's real, or his stamped face
　　Contemplate; what you will, approve,
　　So you will let me love.

10　Alas, alas, who's injured by my love?
　　　What merchant's ships have my sighs drowned?
Who says my tears have overflowed his ground?
　　When did my colds a forward spring remove?
　　　When did the heats which my veins fill
15　　Add one more to the plaguy bill?
Soldiers find wars, and lawyers find out still
　　Litigious men, which quarrels move,
　　Though she and I do love.

Call us what you will, we are made such by love;
20　　Call her one, me another fly,
We are tapers too, and at our own cost die,
　　And we in us find the eagle and the dove,
　　　The phoenix riddle hath more wit
　　　By us; we two being one, are it.
25　So to one neutral thing both sexes fit
　　We die and rise the same, and prove
　　Mysterious by this love.

We can die by it, if not live by love,
    And if unfit for tombs and hearse
30   Our legend be, it will be fit for verse;
    And if no piece of chronicle we prove,
        We'll build in sonnets pretty rooms;
        As well a well wrought urn becomes
    The greatest ashes, as half-acre tombs,
35   And by these hymns, all shall approve
        Us canonized for love:

And thus invoke us; 'You whom reverend love
        Made one another's hermitage;
You, to whom love was peace, that now is rage;
40   Who did the whole world's soul contract, and
           drove
        Into the glasses of your eyes
        (So made such mirrors, and such spies,
That they did all to you epitomize,)
        Countries, towns, courts: beg from above
45   A pattern of your love!'

The Damp

When I am dead, and doctors know not why,
     And my friends' curiosity
Will have me cut up to survey each part,
When they shall find your picture in my heart,
5   You think a sudden damp of love
       Will through all their senses move,
And work on them as me, and so prefer
Your murder, to the name of massacre.

Poor victories; but if you dare be brave,
10   And pleasure in your conquest have,
First kill th' enormous giant, your Disdain,
And let th' enchantress Honour, next be slain,
       And like a Goth and Vandal rise,
       Deface records, and histories
15 Of your own arts and triumphs over men,
And without such advantage kill me then.

For I could muster up as well as you
      My giants, and my witches too,
Which are vast Constancy, and Secretness,
20 But these I neither look for, nor profess;
       Kill me as woman, let me die
       As a mere man; do you but try
Your passive valour, and you shall find then,
Naked you have odds enough of any man.

The Dream

Dear love, for nothing less than thee
Would I have broke this happy dream,
  It was a theme
For reason, much too strong for phantasy,
5 Therefore thou waked'st me wisely; yet
My dream thou brok'st not, but continued'st it:
Thou art so true, that thoughts of thee suffice,
To make dreams truths, and fables histories;
Enter these arms, for since thou thought'st it best,
10 Not to dream all my dream, let's act the rest.

As lightning, or a taper's light,
Thine eyes, and not thy noise waked me;
  Yet I thought thee
(For thou lov'st truth) an angel, at first sight,
15 But when I saw thou saw'st my heart,
And knew'st my thoughts, beyond an angel's art,
When thou knew'st what I dreamed, when thou
  knew'st when
Excess of joy would wake me, and cam'st then,
I must confess, it could not choose but be
20 Profane, to think thee anything but thee.

Coming and staying showed thee, thee,
But rising makes me doubt, that now,
  Thou art not thou.
That love is weak, where fear's as strong as he;
25 'Tis not all spirit, pure, and brave,
If mixture it of fear, shame, honour, have.
Perchance as torches which must ready be,
Men light and put out, so thou deal'st with me,
Thou cam'st to kindle, goest to come; then I
30 Will dream that hope again, but else would die.

The Ecstasy

Where, like a pillow on a bed,
    A pregnant bank swelled up, to rest
The violet's reclining head,
    Sat we two, one another's best;

5   Our hands were firmly cemented
        With a fast balm, which thence did spring,
Our eye-beams twisted, and did thread
        Our eyes, upon one double string;

So to' intergraft our hands, as yet
10   Was all our means to make us one,
And pictures in our eyes to get
        Was all our propagation.

As 'twixt two equal armies, Fate
        Suspends uncertain victory,
15   Our souls, (which to advance their state,
        Were gone out), hung 'twixt her, and me.

And whilst our souls negotiate there,
        We like sepulchral statues lay;
All day, the same our postures were,
20   And we said nothing, all the day.

If any, so by love refined,
        That he soul's language understood,
And by good love were grown all mind,
        Within convenient distance stood,

25 He (though he knew not which soul spake
        Because both meant, both spake the same)
    Might thence a new concoction take,
        And part far purer than he came.

    This ecstasy doth unperplex
30   (We said) and tell us what we love,
    We see by this, it was not sex,
        We see, we saw not what did move:

    But as all several souls contain
        Mixture of things, they know not what,
35 Love, these mixed souls doth mix again,
        And makes both one, each this and that.

    A single violet transplant,
        The strength, the colour, and the size,
    (All which before was poor, and scant,)
40   Redoubles still, and multiplies.

    When love, with one another so
        Interinanimates two souls,
    That abler soul, which thence doth flow,
        Defects of loneliness controls.

45 We then, who are this new soul, know,
        Of what we are composed, and made,
    For, th' atomies of which we grow,
        Are souls, whom no change can invade.

    But O alas, so long, so far
50   Our bodies why do we forbear?
    They are ours, though they are not we, we are
        The intelligences, they the sphere.

We owe them thanks, because they thus,
    Did us, to us, at first convey,
55   Yielded their forces, sense, to us,
    Nor are dross to us, but allay.

On man heaven's influence works not so,
    But that it first imprints the air,
So soul into the soul may flow,
60   Though it to body first repair.

As our blood labours to beget
    Spirits, as like souls as it can,
Because such fingers need to knit
    That subtle knot, which makes us man:

65   So must pure lovers' souls descend
    T' affections, and to faculties,
Which sense may reach and apprehend,
    Else a great prince in prison lies.

To our bodies turn we then, that so
70   Weak men on love revealed may look;
Love's mysteries in souls do grow,
    But yet the body is his book.

And if some lover, such as we,
    Have heard this dialogue of one,
75   Let him still mark us, he shall see
    Small change, when we'are to bodies gone.

The Expiration

So, so, break off this last lamenting kiss,
    Which sucks two souls, and vapours both away,
Turn thou ghost that way, and let me turn this,
    And let ourselves benight our happiest day,
5   We asked none leave to love; nor will we owe
    Any, so cheap a death, as saying, Go;

Go; and if that word have not quite killed thee,
    Ease me with death, by bidding me go too.
Oh, if it have, let my word work on me,
10 And a just office on a murderer do.
Except it be too late, to kill me so,
    Being double dead, going, and bidding, go.

A Fever

Oh do not die, for I shall hate
    All women so, when thou art gone,
That thee I shall not celebrate,
    When I remember, thou wast one.

5   But yet thou canst not die, I know,
    To leave this world behind, is death,
But when thou from this world wilt go,
    The whole world vapours with thy breath.

Or if, when thou, the world's soul, go'st,
10 It stay, 'tis but thy carcase then,
The fairest woman, but thy ghost,
  But corrupt worms, the worthiest men.

Oh wrangling schools, that search what fire
  Shall burn this world, had none the wit
15 Unto this knowledge to aspire,
  That this her fever might be it?

And yet she cannot waste by this,
  Nor long bear this torturing wrong,
For much corruption needful is
20 To fuel such a fever long.

These burning fits but meteors be,
  Whose matter in thee is soon spent.
Thy beauty, and all parts, which are thee,
  Are unchangeable firmament.

25 Yet 'twas of my mind, seizing thee,
  Though it in thee cannot perséver.
For I had rather owner be
  Of thee one hour, than all else ever.

The Flea

Mark but this flea, and mark in this,
How little that which thou deny'st me is;
Me it sucked first, and now sucks thee,
And in this flea, our two bloods mingled be;
5   Confess it, this cannot be said
A sin, or shame, or loss of maidenhead,
      Yet this enjoys before it woo,
      And pampered swells with one blood made of two,
And this, alas, is more than we would do.

10   Oh stay, three lives in one flea spare,
Where we almost, nay more than married are.
This flea is you and I, and this
Our marriage bed, and marriage temple is;
Though parents grudge, and you, we'are met,
15   And cloistered in these living walls of jet.
      Though use make you apt to kill me,
      Let not to this, self murder added be,
      And sacrilege, three sins in killing three.

Cruel and sudden, has thou since
20   Purpled thy nail, in blood of innocence?
In what could this flea guilty be,
Except in that drop which it sucked from thee?
Yet thou triumph'st, and say'st that thou
Find'st not thyself, nor me the weaker now;
25   'Tis true, then learn how false, fears be;
      Just so much honour, when thou yield'st to me,
      Will waste, as this flea's death took life from thee.

The Funeral

Whoever comes to shroud me, do not harm
      Nor question much
That subtle wreath of hair, which crowns my arm;
The mystery, the sign you must not touch,
5   For 'tis my outward soul,
Viceroy to that, which then to heaven being gone,
      Will leave this to control,
And keep these limbs, her provinces, from dissolution.

For if the sinewy thread my brain lets fall
10   Through every part,
Can tie those parts, and make me one of all;
These hairs which upward grew, and strength and art
      Have from a better brain,
Can better do it; except she meant that I
15   By this should know my pain,
As prisoners then are manacled, when they are
      condemned to die.

Whate'er she meant by it, bury it with me,
      For since I am
Love's martyr, it might breed idolatry,
20 If into others' hands these relics came;
      As 'twas humility
To afford to it all that a soul can do,
      So, 'tis some bravery,
That since you would save none of me, I bury some
      of you.

The Good Morrow

I wonder by my troth, what thou, and I
  Did, till we loved? were we not weaned till then,
But sucked on country pleasures, childishly?
  Or snorted we in the seven sleepers' den?
5 'Twas so; but this, all pleasures fancies be.
If ever any beauty I did see,
Which I desired, and got, 'twas but a dream of thee.

And now good morrow to our waking souls,
  Which watch not one another out of fear;
10 For love, all love of other sights controls,
  And makes one little room, an every where.
Let sea-discoverers to new worlds have gone,
Let maps to others, worlds on worlds have shown,
Let us possess one world, each hath one, and is one.

15 My face in thine eye, thine in mine appears,
  And true plain hearts do in the faces rest,
Where can we find two better hemispheres
  Without sharp north, without declining west?
What ever dies, was not mixed equally;
20 If our two loves be one, or, thou and I
Love so alike, that none do slacken, none can die.

A Jet Ring Sent

      Thou art not so black, as my heart,
       Nor half so brittle, as her heart, thou art;
What wouldst thou say? Shall both our properties by
       thee be spoke,
       Nothing more endless, nothing sooner broke?

5   Marriage rings are not of this stuff;
       Oh, why should aught less precious, or less tough
Figure our loves? Except in thy name thou have bid it say,
       I am cheap, and naught but fashion, fling me away.

      Yet stay with me since thou art come,
10   Circle this finger's top, which didst her thumb.
Be justly proud, and gladly safe, that thou dost dwell
       with me,
       She that, oh, broke her faith, would soon break thee.

Lovers' Infiniteness

If yet I have not all thy love,
Dear, I shall never have it all,
I cannot breathe one other sigh, to move,
Nor can entreat one other tear to fall.
5   All my treasure, which should purchase thee,
Sighs, tears, and oaths, and letters I have spent,
Yet no more can be due to me,
Than at the bargain made was meant.
If then thy gift of love were partial,
10 That some to me, some should to others fall,
      Dear, I shall never have thee all.

Or if then thou gavest me all,
All was but all, which thou hadst then;
But if in thy heart, since, there be or shall
15 New love created be, by other men,
Which have their stocks entire, and can in tears,
In sighs, in oaths, and letters outbid me,
This new love may beget new fears,
For, this love was not vowed by thee.
20 And yet it was, thy gift being general,
The ground, thy heart is mine; whatever shall
      Grow there, dear, I should have it all.

Yet I would not have all yet,
He that hath all can have no more,
25 And since my love doth every day admit
New growth, thou shouldst have new rewards in
      store;
Thou canst not every day give me thy heart,
If thou canst give it, then thou never gav'st it:
Love's riddles are, that though thy heart depart,
30 It stays at home, and thou with losing sav'st it:
But we will have a way more liberal,
Than changing hearts, to join them, so we shall
      Be one, and one another's all.

Love's Alchemy

Some that have deeper digged love's mine than I,
Say, where his centric happiness doth lie:
   I have loved, and got, and told,
But should I love, get, tell, till I were old,
5 I should not find that hidden mystery;
   Oh, 'tis imposture all:
And as no chemic yet the elixir got,
   But glorifies his pregnant pot,
   If by the way to him befall
10 Some odoriferous thing, or medicinal,
   So, lovers dream a rich and long delight,
   But get a winter-seeming summer's night.

Our ease, our thrift, our honour, and our day,
Shall we, for this vain bubble's shadow pay?
15   Ends love in this, that my man,
Can be as happy as I can; if he can
Endure the short scorn of a bridegroom's play?
   That loving wretch that swears,
'Tis not the bodies marry, but the minds,
20 Which he in her angelic finds,
Would swear as justly, that he hears,
In that day's rude hoarse minstrelsy, the spheres.
Hope not for mind in women; at their best
   Sweetness and wit, they are but mummy, possessed.

Love's Growth

I scarce believe my love to be so pure
  As I had thought it was,
  Because it doth endure
Vicissitude, and season, as the grass;
5 Methinks I lied all winter, when I swore,
My love was infinite, if spring make it more.
But if this medicine, love, which cures all sorrow
With more, not only be no quintessence,
But mixed of all stuffs, paining soul, or sense,
10 And of the sun his working vigour borrow,
Love's not so pure, and abstract, as they use
To say, which have no mistress but their Muse,
But as all else, being elemented too,
Love sometimes would contemplate, sometimes do.

15 And yet not greater, but more eminent,
  Love by the spring is grown;
  As, in the firmament,
Stars by the sun are not enlarged, but shown,
Gentle love deeds, as blossoms on a bough,
20 From love's awakened root do bud out now.
If, as in water stirred more circles be
Produced by one, love such additions take,
Those like so many spheres, but one heaven make,
For, they are all concentric unto thee,
25 And though each spring do add to love new heat,
As princes do in times of action get
New taxes, and remit them not in peace,
No winter shall abate the spring's increase.

A Nocturnal upon S. Lucy's Day, being the shortest day

'Tis the year's midnight, and it is the day's,
Lucy's, who scarce seven hours herself unmasks,
    The sun is spent, and now his flasks
    Send forth light squibs, no constant rays;
5   The world's whole sap is sunk:
The general balm th' hydroptic earth hath drunk,
Whither, as to the bed's-feet, life is shrunk,
Dead and interred; yet all these seem to laugh,
Compared with me, who am their epitaph.

10 Study me then, you who shall lovers be
At the next world, that is, at the next spring:
    For I am every dead thing,
    In whom love wrought new alchemy.
      For his art did express
15 A quintessence even from nothingness,
From dull privations, and lean emptiness
He ruined me, and I am re-begot
Of absence, darkness, death; things which are not.

All others, from all things, draw all that's good,
20 Life, soul, form, spirit, whence they being have;
    I, by love's limbeck, am the grave
    Of all, that's nothing. Oft a flood
      Have we two wept, and so
Drowned the whole world, us two; oft did we grow
25 To be two chaoses, when we did show
Care to aught else; and often absences
Withdrew our souls, and made us carcases.

But I am by her death (which word wrongs her)
Of the first nothing, the elixir grown;
30   Were I a man, that I were one,
          I needs must know; I should prefer,
            If I were any beast,
Some ends, some means; yea plants, yea stones
          detest,
And love; all, all some properties invest;
35   If I an ordinary nothing were,
As shadow, a light, and body must be here.

But I am none; nor will my sun renew.
You lovers, for whose sake, the lesser sun
          At this time to the Goat is run
40   To fetch new lust, and give it you,
            Enjoy your summer all;
Since she enjoys her long night's festival,
Let me prepare towards her, and let me call
This hour her vigil, and her eve, since this
45   Both the year's, and the day's deep midnight is.

The Relic

When my grave is broke up again
Some second guest to entertain,
(For graves have learned that woman-head
To be to more than one a bed)
5   And he that digs it, spies
A bracelet of bright hair about the bone,
          Will he not let us alone,
And think that there a loving couple lies,
Who thought that this device might be some way
10   To make their souls, at the last busy day,
Meet at this grave, and make a little stay?
          If this fall in a time, or land,
              Where mis-devotion doth command,
              Then, he that digs us up, will bring
15   Us, to the Bishop, and the King,
              To make us relics; then
Thou shalt be a Mary Magdalen, and I
              A something else thereby;
All women shall adore us, and some men;
20   And since at such time, miracles are sought,
I would have that age by this paper taught
What miracles we harmless lovers wrought.

          First, we loved well and faithfully,
              Yet knew not what we loved, nor why,
25   Difference of sex no more we knew,
              Than our guardian angels do;
              Coming and going, we
Perchance might kiss, but not between those meals;
              Our hands ne'er touched the seals,
30   Which nature, injured by late law, sets free:
These miracles we did; but now alas,
All measure, and all language, I should pass,
Should I tell what a miracle she was.

Song

Go, and catch a falling star,
　　　Get with child a mandrake root,
Tell me, where all past years are,
　　　Or who cleft the Devil's foot,
5　Teach me to hear mermaids singing,
　　　Or to keep off envy's stinging,
　　　　And find
　　　　What wind
Serves to advance an honest mind.

10　If thou be'est born to strange sights,
　　　Things invisible to see,
Ride ten thousand days and nights,
　　　Till age snow white hairs on thee,
Thou, when thou return'st, wilt tell me
15　All strange wonders that befell thee,
　　　　And swear
　　　　No where
Lives a woman true, and fair.

If thou find'st one, let me know,
20　　Such a pilgrimage were sweet,
Yet do not, I would not go,
　　　Though at next door we might meet,
Though she were true, when you met her,
And last, till you write your letter,
25　　　Yet she
　　　　Will be
False, ere I come, to two, or three.

Song

Sweetest love, I do not go,
    For weariness of thee,
Nor in hope the world can show
    A fitter love for me;
5   But since that I
Must die at last, 'tis best,
To use my self in jest
        Thus by feigned deaths to die.

Yesternight the sun went hence,
10   And yet is here today,
He hath no desire nor sense,
    Nor half so short a way:
        Then fear not me,
But believe that I shall make
15 Speedier journeys, since I take
        More wings and spurs than he.

O how feeble is man's power,
    That if good fortune fall,
Cannot add another hour,
20   Nor a lost hour recall!
        But come bad chance,
And we join to it our strength,
And we teach it art and length,
        Itself o'er us to advance.

25 When thou sigh'st, thou sigh'st not wind,
    But sigh'st my soul away,
When thou weep'st, unkindly kind,
    My life's blood doth decay.

It cannot be
30   That thou lov'st me, as thou say'st,
If in thine my life thou waste,
        Thou art the best of me.

Let not thy divining heart
        Forethink me any ill,
35   Destiny may take thy part,
        And may thy fears fulfil;
        But think that we
Are but turned aside to sleep;
They who one another keep
40   Alive, ne'er parted be.

The Sun Rising

Busy old fool, unruly sun,
        Why dost thou thus,
Through windows, and through curtains call on us?
Must to thy motions lovers' seasons run?
5   Saucy pedantic wretch, go chide
        Late school-boys, and sour prentices,
        Go tell court-huntsmen, that the King will ride,
        Call country ants to harvest offices;
Love, all alike, no season knows, nor clime,
10   Nor hours, days, months, which are the rags of time.

Thy beams, so reverend, and strong
        Why shouldst thou think?
I could eclipse and cloud them with a wink,
But that I would not lose her sight so long:
15   If her eyes have not blinded thine,

Look, and tomorrow late, tell me,
Whether both th'Indias of spice and mine
Be where thou left'st them, or lie here with me.
Ask for those kings whom thou saw'st yesterday,
20   And thou shalt hear, All here in one bed lay.

She'is all states, and all princes, I,
Nothing else is.
Princes do but play us; compared to this,
All honour's mimic; all wealth alchemy.
25   Thou sun art half as happy as we,
In that the world's contracted thus;
Thine age asks ease, and since thy duties be
To warm the world, that's done in warming us.
Shine here to us, and thou art everywhere;
30   This bed thy centre is, these walls, thy sphere.

The Triple Fool

I am two fools, I know,
For loving, and for saying so
In whining poetry;
But where's that wiseman, that would not be I,
5   If she would not deny?
Then as th'earth's inward narrow crooked lanes
Do purge sea water's fretful salt away,
I thought, if I could draw my pains
Through rhyme's vexation, I should them allay.
10   Grief brought to numbers cannot be so fierce,
For, he tames it, that fetters it in verse

> But when I have done so,
> Some man, his art and voice to show,
> Doth set and sing my pain,
> And, by delighting many, frees again
> Grief, which verse did restrain.
> To love and grief tribute of verse belongs,
> But not of such as pleases when 'tis read,
> Both are increased by such songs:
> For both their triumphs so are published,
> And I, which was two fools, do so grow three;
> Who are a little wise, the best fools be.

15

20

Twicknam Garden

> Blasted with sighs, and surrounded with tears,
> Hither I come to seek the spring,
> And at mine eyes, and at mine ears,
> Receive such balms, as else cure everything;
> But O, self traitor, I do bring
> The spider love, which transubstantiates all,
> And can convert manna to gall,
> And that this place may thoroughly be thought
> True paradise, I have the serpent brought.

5

> 'Twere wholesomer for me, that winter did
> Benight the glory of this place,
> And that a grave frost did forbid
> These trees to laugh, and mock me to my face;
> But that I may not this disgrace
> Endure, nor yet leave loving, Love, let me
> Some senseless piece of this place be;
> Make me a mandrake, so I may groan here,
> Or a stone fountain weeping out my year.

10

15

Hither with crystal vials, lovers come,
20   And take my tears, which are love's wine,
And try your mistress' tears at home,
      For all are false, that taste not just like mine;
      Alas, hearts do not in eyes shine,
Nor can you more judge woman's thoughts by tears,
25   Than by her shadow, what she wears.
O perverse sex, where none is true but she,
      Who's therefore true, because her truth kills me.

The Undertaking

I have done one braver thing
      Than all the Worthies did,
And yet a braver thence doth spring,
      Which is, to keep that hid.

5   It were but madness now t'impart
      The skill of specular stone,
When he which can have learned the art
      To cut it, can find none.

So, if I now should utter this,
10   Others (because no more
Such stuff to work upon, there is,)
      Would love but as before.

But he who loveliness within
      Hath found, all outward loathes,
15   For he who colour loves, and skin,
      Loves but their oldest clothes.

If, as I have, you also do
    Virtue attired in woman see,
And dare love that, and say so too,
20   And forget the He and She;

And if this love, though placed so,
    From profane men you hide,
Which will no faith on this bestow,
    Or, if they do, deride:

25   Then you have done a braver thing
    Than all the Worthies did,
And a braver thence will spring,
    Which is, to keep that hid.

A Valediction: forbidding Mourning

As virtuous men pass mildly away,
    And whisper to their souls, to go,
Whilst some of their sad friends do say,
    The breath goes now, and some say, no:

5   So let us melt, and make no noise,
    No tear-floods, nor sigh-tempests move,
'Twere profanation of our joys
    To tell the laity our love.

Moving of th' earth brings harms and fears,
10   Men reckon what it did and meant,
But trepidation of the spheres,
    Though greater far, is innocent.

Dull sublunary lovers' love
    (Whose soul is sense) cannot admit
15   Absence, because it doth remove
    Those things which elemented it.

But we by a love, so much refined,
    That our selves know not what it is,
Inter-assured of the mind,
20   Care less, eyes, lips, and hands to miss.

Our two souls therefore, which are one,
    Though I must go, endure not yet
A breach, but an expansion,
    Like gold to aery thinness beat.

25   If they be two, they are two so
    As stiff twin compasses are two,
Thy soul the fixed foot, makes no show
    To move, but doth, if th'other do.

And though it in the centre sit,
30   Yet when the other far doth roam,
It leans, and hearkens after it,
    And grows erect, as that comes home.

Such wilt thou be to me, who must
    Like th' other foot, obliquely run;
35   Thy firmness makes my circle just,
    And makes me end, where I begun.

A Valediction: of Weeping

   Let me pour forth
My tears before thy face, whilst I stay here,
For thy face coins them, and thy stamp they bear,
And by this mintage they are something worth,
5   For thus they be
    Pregnant of thee;
Fruits of much grief they are, emblems of more,
When a tear falls, that thou falls which it bore,
So thou and I are nothing then, when on a divers shore.

10   On a round ball
A workman that hath copies by, can lay
An Europe, Afric, and an Asia,
And quickly make that, which was nothing, all,
    So doth each tear,
15   Which thee doth wear,
A globe, yea world by that impression grow,
Till thy tears mixed with mine do overflow
This world, by waters sent from thee, my heaven dissolved so

   O more than moon,
20 Draw not up seas to drown me in thy sphere,
Weep me not dead, in thine arms, but forbear
To teach the sea, what it may do too soon;
    Let not the wind
    Example find,
25 To do me more harm, than it purposeth;
Since thou and I sigh one another's breath,
Whoe'er sighs most, is cruellest, and hastes the other's death.

Woman's Constancy

Now thou hast loved me one whole day,
Tomorrow when thou leav'st, what wilt thou say?
Wilt thou then antedate some new made vow?
    Or say that now
5   We are not just those persons, which we were?
Or, that oaths made in reverential fear
Of Love, and his wrath, any may forswear?
Or, as true deaths, true marriages untie,
So lovers' contracts, images of those,
10   Bind but till sleep, death's image, them unloose?
    Or, your own end to justify,
For having purposed change, and falsehood, you
Can have no way but falsehood to be true?
Vain lunatic, against these 'scapes I could
15   Dispute, and conquer, if I would,
        Which I abstain to do,
For by tomorrow, I may think so too.

Elegies

Elegy 4: The Perfume

Once, and but once found in thy company,
All thy supposed escapes are laid on me;
And as a thief at bar, is questioned there
By all the men, that have been robbed that year,
So am I, (by this traitorous means surprised)
By thy hydroptic father catechized.
Though he had wont to search with glazed eyes,
As though he came to kill a cockatrice,
Though he have oft sworn, that he would remove
Thy beauty's beauty, and food of our love,
Hope of his goods, if I with thee were seen,
Yet close and secret, as our souls, we have been.
Though thy immortal mother which doth lie
Still buried in her bed, yet will not die,
Takes this advantage to sleep out day-light,
And watch thy entries, and returns all night,
And, when she takes thy hand, and would seem kind,
Doth search what rings, and armlets she can find,
And kissing notes the colour of thy face,
And fearing less thou art swoll'n, doth thee embrace;
To try if thou long, doth name strange meats,
And notes thy paleness, blushing, sighs, and sweats;
And politicly will to thee confess
The sins of her own youth's rank lustiness;
Yet love these sorceries did remove, and move
Thee to gull thine own mother for my love.
Thy little brethren, which like faery sprites
Oft skipped into our chamber, those sweet nights,
And kissed, and ingled on thy father's knee,
Were bribed next day, to tell what they did see.

The grim eight-foot-high iron-bound serving-man,
That oft names God in oaths, and only then,
He that to bar the first gate, doth as wide
As the great Rhodian Colossus stride,
35 Which, if in hell no other pains there were,
Makes me fear hell, because he must be there:
Though by thy father he were hired to this,
Could never witness any touch or kiss.
But Oh, too common ill, I brought with me
40 That, which betrayed me to mine enemy:
A loud perfume, which at my entrance cried
Even at thy father's nose, so we were spied.
When, like a tyrant king, that in his bed
Smelt gunpowder, the pale wretch shivered.
45 Had it been some bad smell, he would have thought
That his own feet, or breath, that smell had wrought.
But as we in our isle imprisoned,
Where cattle only, and diverse dogs are bred,
The precious unicorns, strange monsters call,
50 So thought he good, strange, that had none at all.
I taught my silks, their whistling to forbear,
Even my oppressed shoes, dumb and speechless were,
Only, thou bitter sweet, whom I had laid
Next me, me traitorously hast betrayed,
55 And unsuspected hast invisibly
At once fled unto him, and stayed with me.
Base excrement of earth, which dost confound
Sense, from distinguishing the sick from sound;
By thee the silly amorous sucks his death
60 By drawing in a leprous harlot's breath;
By thee, the greatest stain to man's estate
Falls on us, to be called effeminate;
Though you be much loved in the prince's hall,
There, things that seem, exceed substantial.
65 Gods, when ye fumed on altars, were pleased well,

Because you were burnt, not that they liked your
    smell;
You are loathsome all, being taken simply alone,
Shall we love ill things joined, and hate each one?
If you were good, your good doth soon decay;
70   And you are rare, that takes the good away.
All my perfumes, I give most willingly
To embalm thy father's corse; What? will he die?

Elegy 5: His Picture

Here take my picture, though I bid farewell;
Thine, in my heart, where my soul dwells, shall
    dwell.
'Tis like me now, but I dead, 'twill be more
When we are shadows both, than 'twas before.
5   When weather-beaten I come back; my hand,
Perhaps with rude oars torn, or sun-beams tanned,
My face and breast of haircloth, and my head
With care's rash sudden hoariness o'erspread,
My body a sack of bones, broken within,
10   And powder's blue stains scattered on my skin;
If rival fools tax thee to have loved a man,
So foul, and coarse, as oh, I may seem then,
This shall say what I was: and thou shalt say,
Do his hurts reach me? doth my worth decay?
15   Or do they reach his judging mind, that he
Should now love less, what he did love to see?
That which in him was fair and delicate,
Was but the milk, which in love's childish state
Did nurse it: who now is grown strong enough
20   To feed on that, which to disused tastes seems tough.

Elegy 16: On his Mistress

By our first strange and fatal interview,
By all desires which thereof did ensue,
By our long starving hopes, by that remorse
Which my words' masculine persuasive force
5 Begot in thee, and by the memory
Of hurts, which spies and rivals threatened me,
I calmly beg: but by thy father's wrath,
By all pains, which want and divorcement hath,
I conjure thee; and all the oaths which I
10 And thou have sworn to seal joint constancy,
Here I unswear, and overswear them thus,
Thou shalt not love by ways so dangerous.
Temper, O fair love, love's impetuous rage,
Be my true mistress still, not my feigned page;
15 I'll go, and, by thy kind leave, leave behind
Thee, only worthy to nurse in my mind
Thirst to come back; oh, if thou die before,
From other lands my soul towards thee shall soar,
Thy (else almighty) beauty cannot move
20 Rage from the seas, nor thy love teach them love,
Nor tame wild Boreas' harshness; thou hast read
How roughly he in pieces shivered
Fair Orithea, whom he swore he loved.
Fall ill or good, 'tis madness to have proved
25 Dangers unurged; feed on this flattery,
That absent lovers one in th' other be.
Dissemble nothing, not a boy, nor change
Thy body's habit, nor mind's; be not strange
To thy self only; all will spy in thy face
30 A blushing womanly discovering grace;
Richly clothed apes, are called apes, and as soon

Eclipsed as bright we call the moon the moon.
Men of France, changeable chameleons,
Spitals of diseases, shops of fashions,
35   Love's fuellers, and the rightest company
Of players, which upon the world's stage be,
Will quickly know thee, and know thee; and alas
Th' indifferent Italian, as we pass
His warm land, well content to think thee page,
40   Will hunt thee with such lust, and hideous rage,
As Lot's fair guests were vexed. But none of these
Nor spongy hydroptic Dutch shall thee displease,
If thou stay here. Oh stay here, for, for thee
England is only a worthy gallery,
45   To walk in expectation, till from thence
Our greatest King call thee to his presence.
When I am gone, dream me some happiness,
Nor let thy looks our long-hid love confess,
Nor praise, nor dispraise me, nor bless nor curse
50   Openly love's force, nor in bed fright thy nurse
With midnight's startings, crying out, 'Oh, oh
Nurse, O my love is slain, I saw him go
O'er the white Alps alone; I saw him, I,
Assailed, fight, taken, stabbed, bleed, fall, and die.'
55   Augur me better chance, except dread Jove
Think it enough for me to have had thy love.

Elegy 19: To his Mistress Going to Bed

Come, Madam, come, all rest my powers defy,
Until I labour, I in labour lie.
The foe oft-times having the foe in sight,

Is tried with standing though he never fight.
5   Off with that girdle, like heaven's zone glistering,
But a far fairer world encompassing.
Unpin that spangled breastplate which you wear,
That th' eyes of busy fools may be stopped there.
Unlace yourself, for that harmonious chime
10   Tells me from you, that now 'tis your bed time.
Off with that happy busk, which I envy,
That still can be, and still can stand so nigh.
Your gown going off, such beauteous state reveals,
As when from flowery meads th' hill's shadow steals.
15   Off with that wiry coronet and show
The hairy diadem which on you doth grow;
Now off with those shoes, and then safely tread
In this love's hallowed temple, this soft bed.
In such white robes heaven's angels used to be
20   Received by men; thou angel bring'st with thee
A heaven like Mahomet's paradise; and though
Ill spirits walk in white, we easily know
By this these angels from an evil sprite,
Those set our hairs, but these our flesh upright.
25   License my roving hands, and let them go
Before, behind, between, above, below.
O my America, my new found land,
My kingdom, safeliest when with one man manned,
My mine of precious stones, my empery,
30   How blessed am I in this discovering thee!
To enter in these bonds, is to be free;
Then where my hand is set, my seal shall be.
      Full nakedness, all joys are due to thee.
As souls unbodied, bodies unclothed must be,
35   To taste whole joys. Gems which you women use
Are like Atlanta's balls, cast in men's views,
That when a fool's eye lighteth on a gem,

His earthly soul may covet theirs, not them.
Like pictures, or like books' gay coverings made
40 For laymen, are all women thus arrayed;
Themselves are mystic books, which only we
Whom their imputed grace will dignify
Must see revealed. Then since I may know,
As liberally, as to a midwife, show
45 Thyself: cast all, yea, this white linen hence,
Here is no penance, much less innocence.
    To teach thee, I am naked first, why then
What needst thou have more covering than a man.

Religious Poems

Holy Sonnets

6

This is my play's last scene, here heavens appoint
My pilgrimage's last mile; and my race
Idly, yet quickly run, hath this last pace,
My span's last inch, my minute's latest point,
5   And gluttonous death, will instantly unjoint
My body, and soul, and I shall sleep a space,
But my'ever-waking part shall see that face,
Whose fear already shakes my every joint:
Then, as my soul, to heaven her first seat, takes flight,
10 And earth-born body, in the earth shall dwell,
So, fall my sins, that all may have their right,
To where they are bred, and would press me, to hell.
Impute me righteous, thus purged of evil,
For thus I leave the world, the flesh, and devil.

7

At the round earth's imagined corners, blow
Your trumpets, angels, and arise, arise
From death, you numberless infinities
Of souls, and to your scattered bodies go,
5   All whom the flood did, and fire shall o'erthrow,
All whom war, dearth, age, agues, tyrannies,
Despair, law, chance, hath slain, and you whose eyes,
Shall behold God, and never taste death's woe.
But let them sleep, Lord, and me mourn a space,
10 For, if above all these, my sins abound,
'Tis late to ask abundance of thy grace,
When we are there; here on this lowly ground,
Teach me how to repent; for that's as good
As if thou hadst sealed my pardon, with thy blood.

10

Death be not proud, though some have called thee
Mighty and dreadful, for, thou art not so,
For, those, whom thou think'st, thou dost
    overthrow,
Die not, poor death, nor yet canst thou kill me;
5 From rest and sleep, which but thy pictures be,
Much pleasure, then from thee, much more must
    flow,
And soonest our best men with thee do go,
Rest of their bones, and soul's delivery.
Thou art slave to fate, chance, kings, and desperate
    men,
10 And dost with poison, war, and sickness dwell,
And poppy, or charms can make us sleep as well,
And better than thy stroke; why swell'st thou then?
One short sleep past, we wake eternally,
And death shall be no more, Death thou shalt die.

13

What if this present were the world's last night?
Mark in my heart, O soul, where thou dost dwell,
The picture of Christ crucified, and tell
Whether that countenance can thee affright,
5 Tears in his eyes quench the amazing light,
Blood fills his frowns, which from his pierced head
    fell,
And can that tongue adjudge thee unto hell,
Which prayed forgiveness for his foes' fierce spite?
No, no; but as in my idolatry
10 I said to all my profane mistresses,
Beauty, of pity, foulness only is
A sign of rigour: so I say to thee,
To wicked spirits are horrid shapes assigned,
This beauteous form assures a piteous mind.

14

Batter my heart, three-personed God; for, you
As yet but knock, breathe, shine, and seek to mend;
That I may rise, and stand, o'erthrow me, and bend
Your force, to break, blow, burn, and make me new.
5   I, like an usurped town, to another due,
Labour to admit you, but oh, to no end,
Reason your viceroy in me, me should defend,
But is captived, and proves weak or untrue,
Yet dearly'I love you, and would be loved fain,
10 But am betrothed unto your enemy,
Divorce me, untie, or break that knot again,
Take me to you, imprison me, for I
Except you enthral me, never shall be free,
Nor ever chaste, except you ravish me.

17

Since she whom I loved hath paid her last debt
To nature, and to hers, and my good is dead,
And her soul early into heaven ravished,
Wholly in heavenly things my mind is set.
5   Here the admiring her my mind did whet
To seek thee God; so streams do show the head,
But though I have found thee, and thou my thirst
    hast fed,
A holy thirsty dropsy melts me yet.
But why should I beg more love, when as thou
10 Dost woo my soul for hers; offering all thine:
And dost not only fear lest I allow
My love to saints and angels, things divine,
But in thy tender jealousy dost doubt
Lest the world, flesh, yea Devil put thee out.

19

Oh, to vex me, contraries meet in one:
Inconstancy unnaturally hath begot
A constant habit; that when I would not
I change in vows, and in devotion.
5   As humorous is my contrition
As my profane love, and as soon forgot:
As riddlingly distempered, cold and hot,
As praying, as mute; as infinite, as none.
I durst not view heaven yesterday; and today
10   In prayers, and flattering speeches I court God:
Tomorrow I quake with true fear of his rod.
So my devout fits come and go away
Like a fantastic ague: save that here
Those are my best days, when I shake with fear.

Good Friday, 1613. Riding Westward

Let man's soul be a sphere, and then, in this,
The intelligence that moves, devotion is,
And as the other spheres, by being grown
Subject to foreign motions, lose their own,
5   And being by others hurried every day,
Scarce in a year their natural form obey:
Pleasure or business, so, our souls admit
For their first mover, and are whirled by it.
Hence is't, that I am carried towards the west
10 This day, when my soul's form bends toward the east.
There I should see a sun, by rising set,
And by that setting endless day beget;
But that Christ on this Cross, did rise and fall,

Sin had eternally benighted all.
15 Yet dare I'almost be glad, I do not see
That spectacle of too much weight for me.
Who sees God's face, that is self life, must die;
What a death were it then to see God die?
It made his own lieutenant Nature shrink,
20 It made his footstool crack, and the sun wink.
Could I behold those hands which span the poles,
And turn all spheres at once, pierced with those holes?
Could I behold that endless height which is
Zenith to us, and to'our antipodes,
25 Humbled below us? or that blood which is
The seat of all our souls, if not of his,
Made dirt of dust, or that flesh which was worn,
By God, for his apparel, ragged, and torn?
If on these things I durst not look, durst I
30 Upon his miserable mother cast mine eye,
Who was God's partner here, and furnished thus
Half of that sacrifice, which ransomed us?
Though these things, as I ride, be from mine eye,
They are present yet unto my memory,
35 For that looks towards them; and thou look'st
      towards me,
O Saviour, as thou hang'st upon the tree;
I turn my back to thee, but to receive
Corrections, till thy mercies bid thee leave.
O think me worth thine anger, punish me,
40 Burn off my rusts, and my deformity,
Restore thine image, so much, by thy grace,
That thou mayst know me, and I'll turn my face.

A Hymn to Christ, at the Author's last going into Germany

In what torn ship soever I embark,
That ship shall be my emblem of thy ark;
What sea soever swallow me, that flood
Shall be to me an emblem of thy blood;
5   Though thou with clouds of anger do disguise
Thy face; yet through that mask I know those eyes,
    Which, though they turn away sometimes,
      They never will despise.

I sacrifice this Island unto thee,
10   And all whom I loved there, and who loved me;
When I have put our seas twixt them and me,
Put thou thy sea betwixt my sins and thee.
As the tree's sap doth seek the root below
In winter, in my winter now I go,
15   Where none but thee, th' eternal root
      Of true love I may know.

Nor thou nor thy religion dost control,
The amorousness of an harmonious soul,
But thou wouldst have that love thyself: as thou
20   Art jealous, Lord, so I am jealous now,
Thou lov'st not, till from loving more, thou free
My soul; who ever gives, takes liberty:
      O, if thou car'st not whom I love
        Alas, thou lov'st not me.

25   Seal then this bill of my divorce to all,
On whom those fainter beams of love did fall;
Marry those loves, which in youth scattered be
On fame, wit, hopes (false mistresses) to thee.
Churches are best for prayer, that have least light:
30   To see God only, I go out of sight:
        And to 'scape stormy days, I choose
        An everlasting night.

Hymn to God my God, in my Sickness

Since I am coming to that holy room,
    Where, with thy choir of saints for evermore,
I shall be made thy music; as I come
    I tune the instrument here at the door,
5   And what I must do then, think here before.

Whilst my physicians by their love are grown
    Cosmographers, and I their map, who lie
Flat on this bed, that by them may be shown
    That this is my south-west discovery
10   *Per fretum febris*, by these straits to die,

I joy, that in these straits, I see my west;
    For, though their currents yield return to none,
What shall my west hurt me? As west and east
    In all flat maps (and I am one) are one,
15   So death doth touch the resurrection.

Is the Pacific Sea my home? Or are
    The eastern riches? Is Jerusalem?
Anyan, and Magellan, and Gibraltar,
    All straits, and none but straits, are ways to them,
20   Whether where Japhet dwelt, or Cham, or Shem.

We think that Paradise and Calvary,
    Christ's Cross, and Adam's tree, stood in one
        place;
Look Lord, and find both Adams met in me;
    As the first Adam's sweat surrounds my face,
25   May the last Adam's blood my soul embrace.

So, in his purple wrapped receive me Lord,
    By these his thorns give me his other crown;
And as to others' souls I preached thy word,
    Be this my text, my sermon to mine own,
30   Therefore that he may raise the Lord throws down.

A Hymn to God the Father

I
Wilt thou forgive that sin where I begun,
    Which was my sin, though it were done before?
Wilt thou forgive that sin, through which I run,
    And do run still: though still I do deplore?
5   When thou hast done, thou hast not done,
        For, I have more.

II
Wilt thou forgive that sin which I have won
    Others to sin? and, made my sin their door?
Wilt thou forgive that sin which I did shun
10   A year, or two: but wallowed in, a score?
      When thou hast done, thou hast not done,
        For I have more.

III
I have a sin of fear, that when I have spun
    My last thread, I shall perish on the shore;
15 But swear by thy self, that at my death thy son
    Shall shine as he shines now, and heretofore;
      And, having done that, thou hast done,
        I fear no more.

Explanatory Notes

Air and Angels

In language as delicately insubstantial as its subject matter, Donne meditates on souls, light, love, a shapeless flame and angels. The music of its cadences and textures is appropriately airy and refined. The argument emerges so easily out of the varied and, in some cases, surprising imagery, the reader is carried to the conclusion (by no means an uncontroversial one) with a persuasive naturalness.

The argument of the poem is elusive. Those who wish to follow it closely should read the discussions in Helen Gardner's *The Business of Criticism* and Theodore Redpath's summary in his edition of *The Songs and Sonnets of John Donne*, 1956.

Title   It was a problem for medieval theology as to how angels, which are pure spirit, can become visible. Donne depends on the idea that they form bodies out of the air, because the air, while not as pure in substance as angels, is the purest of all the elements.

  1   **Twice or thrice**   Here, and throughout the poem, the reader should attend to the rhymes, repetitions of sounds and textures to appreciate the poem's sound world. Perhaps the verbal music is the enactment of the poem's interest in purity of substances.

  2   **Before I knew**   the same idea is present in *The Good Morrow* (6–7).

  4   **affect**   influence.
       worshipped   adored and honoured. In contemporary love poetry, a beloved was an object of devotion and worship.

  5   **still**   on every occasion.

  6   **lovely glorious nothing**   listen to the note of wonder that runs through the poem.

7–8   The soul needs a body through which it can act. Donne is reversing Platonism. Plato taught that we should search for the Ideal Forms rather than concentrate on this or that particular object. Donne, however, says he has found the concrete embodiment of the Ideal Form of woman.

9 **subtle** a word concerned with refined and rarefied substances. In lines 23–4 angels take bodies of air, because it is the most pure and subtle of material substances.

10 **take a body too** Platonism looks through bodies to Ideal Forms; Donne says that love must find a form – the flesh and blood of a human body – that can be the object of its loving.

11–12 The image is of the lover asking love what kind of a person his hitherto only glimpsed beloved is. Do you find the touch of courtesy – the lover asking a favour of love – appropriate?

13 **assume** at least two ideas are present here. To assume is to take, in the sense that a soul takes a body in order to express itself. The word also means to be taken up into heaven. Perhaps the point is that heaven for the poet is to see the woman, who embodies all that he has ever longed for.
allow to recognize and accept as true.

14 **lip, eye, and brow** The reversal of Platonism (see Notes on 7–8 and 10) will only convince the reader if these lines express the wonder of discovery. See also *A Valediction: forbidding Mourning* (20).

15 **ballast** weights carried in a ship so it can sail more steadily (16) and avoid capsizing. Does anything earlier in the poem prepare us for this surprising image?

17 **wares** goods carried by a ship.

18 **pinnace** a swift, light ship, so one that might easily be overloaded (*overfraught*).

19–20 This probably means: even every single one of your hairs overwhelms me. Is this one of the most wondering and loving lines in the entire poem?

20 **fitter** more appropriate. This word introduces the final stage of the argument. Try to trace the entire movement of the argument in terms of the implicit images of reaching down for a body and reaching up for a refined love.

22 **Extreme, and scatt'ring bright** Is this a good description of Donne's poems?
inhere remain united with.

23–4 See Title note about how angels make themselves visible.

25 Donne argues that his love will be the Intelligence that guides and moves the sphere of a planet or the sun. See *The Ecstasy* (51–2).

25–8 Is it possible to avoid the implication that male love is active and female love passive? If it is not, might some find the close of the poem disappointing?

The Anniversary

Think about how the buoyancy and triumph of the poem's rhythms enforce two of its themes: the superiority of lovers over common humanity and the relationship between love and time. Is the second verse a problem? Do you find it disappointingly flat after the exhilarating opening, or are you impressed because the playful attitude to time has given way to a serious recognition of the inevitability of death?

1 **favourites** courtiers who are favoured by the King. Might this implicit dismissal of the court mean that it is less satisfying than the world of mutual love, or can it be that the poet is creating a compensatory world of mutual love because the court has rejected him?

2 **honours... wits** *honours* are either judges or privileges; *wits* are intellectuals.

7–8 These lines contrast the triumphant close of the poem, in which love is numbered in years (29–30). What might this interesting tension show us about the movement of Donne's mind and the experience of being in love?

9 **Running... runs** think about how the grammatical difference between the participle *running* and the verb *runs* makes a distinction between permanence and change.

10 **first, last, everlasting day** the first day of creation, the day of judgement and eternity.

11 **corse** corpse.

12 **divorce** are the lovers married? As the word *divorce* only applies to those who have been married, we may assume so. But if they are married, why would they be buried in two graves? Perhaps we have to consider the grisly idea that if they had shared one grave, their souls would have been reluctant to leave their decaying corpses on the day of judgement.

15–20 These lines, as is often the case in Donne, are divided between his wonder at the body (think about the lingering regret of leaving *these eyes, and ears,* line 15) and the hope, caught in an unexpected rhyme, of a *love increased there above* (19). In the light of the metaphors associated with occupation – an owner *dwells* but lodgers are *inmates* – think about the relationship between the soul, the body and the grave.

18 **prove** experience will show it to be true.

21 **throughly** thoroughly, completely.

23 **Here upon earth** do these words show what chiefly interests the poet, and if so, what is to be made of the second stanza with its vision of a love perfected in heaven?

25 **Who is so safe as we?** does this rhetorical question work because the reader sees that lovers are significantly different from kings, or is it bravado trying to counter a real doubt that they might not be safe? A similar question can be asked of *Treason* (26).

27 **True and false fears** what is to be feared – time or unfaithfulness? It is also problematic as to which is the *true* and which the *false* fear.

29 **Years and years unto years** do the rhythms of this line emphasize the glorious character of their noble reign in the kingdom of love, or is there a hint of the grinding repetitiveness of passing years?

30 **threescore** since the span of life is usually said to be threescore years and ten (seventy years), is the idea that the lovers are so superior that their reign lasts longer? If so, is the image of aged lovers disconcerting?

The Apparition

One of the teasing things about this dramatic poem is its tone: is it one of vitriolic rage or that of someone who relishes the grotesque comedy of a ghost succeeding in reaching the woman's bed, when the living man did not? The language of crime, guilt and repentance is likewise ambivalent. The problem of tone also touches on the issue of how the poem might be performed: the reader will have to decide whether words such as *When* (1), *Then* (4) (6) and *since my love is spent* (15) should be read with anger or amused playfulness.

3 **solicitation**   the act of earnestly requesting or begging something.

5 **vestal**   vestal virgins were Roman women who lived chaste lives of dedicated religious service.

6 **taper**   candle.

10 **shrink**   does this mean more than the act of a tired lover recoiling from a sexually-demanding woman?

11 **aspen**   a type of poplar noted for the way its leaves tremble in the wind.

12 **quicksilver**   there may be a hint of poison here, as mercury vapour was known to be poisonous.

13 **A verier ghost**   even more of a ghost.

15 **and since my love is spent**   this seems to contradict the opening line, where the poet envisages himself as dead from unrequited love. Is he really in love and hoping that these words will make her submit to him? Is his desire for revenge stronger than his love? Is he pretending to love so that she might feel guilty? Whatever the answer, the inconsistency between (1) and (15) underlines the ambivalence of the poet's attitude. There may be a suggestion of ejaculation in *spent*.

Break of Day

The voice of the poem is a woman. Readers may wonder whether Donne has deliberately fashioned a female voice or whether it is argument rather than gender that interests him. Perhaps the pleading (even beguiling) tone is consciously female. But then, readers might think that the reasons the woman so cleverly urges make it not unlike *Woman's Constancy*. Perhaps *Break of Day* does not have the dismissive gusto of *Woman's Constancy*, but it shares with that poem a delight in agile reasoning.

Title Women requesting the lover not to leave after a night together
is a theme going back to late medieval love poetry. Juliet's plea
to Romeo shows how strong the tradition was.

1 **'Tis true** as in the case of other Donne poems (*The Flea*, for
instance), this is presented as a conversation in which the reader
only hears one voice.

3–4 Do we enjoy her frank admission that they did not go to bed
because it was night?

7 **light** in literature, light is sometimes used to expose
wickedness. Is there a touch of guilt here?

12 **that had them** the meaning seems to be that in having her, the
lover now has the honour that was once hers. What is her
attitude? Is she now dependent upon him, or is there an
attractive boldness in her acceptance that, in the traditional
sense, her honour was lost with her virginity?

16 **busied man** do we see that he is making excuses to leave her
or that she is cleverly portraying him as a small-minded man,
preoccupied with trivial matters?

18 **married man** is there a suggestion here that the man is
adulterous?

The Canonization

This could be called a retirement poem, in that the poet
vehemently scorns the public world and opts, instead, for an
intimate world of love. (Some scholars have speculated that
Donne wrote it in the early years of his marriage, when, due largely
to the hostility of his father-in-law, his future was in question.)
This might account for how the poet both recognizes the
uncertainty of the world yet considers its dangers with amused
detachment. But if it is about retirement, why does the poem close
with the lovers as objects of adoration by *all* (35)? Two further
questions are whether, for all its religious language, the poem
actually celebrates an entirely earthly love, and whether the poem's
changing emotional life matters more than the poem's argument.

Title The central idea of the poem is that the lovers have been canonized – declared to be saints – *for love* (36). This could mean that their love has a mysterious and unearthly quality, or that they have been martyred by those who have excluded them from the public world, or that their loving has been so vigorous they have become martyrs by wearing themselves out.

1 This colloquial outburst (and many other lines) are remarkable for the abruptness of their speech rhythms. A reading of the poem might help you to discover how its emotional and intellectual life is dependent upon these speech rhythms and, also, which are the poem's most crucial words.

2 **palsy… gout** *palsy* is trembling or paralysis; *gout* a disease affecting the joints, commonly associated with old men.

4–9 The emotional cross-currents of these lines might make us wonder about the poet's attitudes. Does he scornfully dismiss the disturber and the public world with the fierce conviction of a moralist or are there elements of fascination, perhaps even of envy, in the way he quickly scans such worldly concerns as commerce, learning, society and the court? A clue might be found by considering the force of the carefully placed verbs – *Take… get… Observe… Contemplate*: do they suggest purposeful activity that is the envy of the poet, or is there something comically mechanical about their frenetic busyness?

6 **Honour… Grace** a Lord and a Bishop or Archbishop.

7 **stamped face** a coin bearing the king's head. (The language of economics is a recurring feature of the poem.)

10–18 What is the poet's attitude in this stanza? If there is scorn in his voice, is it still directed at the disturber, or is his real target those Petrarchan love poets who write of lovers' tears drowning the world or their sighs creating storms? Alternatively, is the poet actually revelling in poetic exaggeration?

20 **fly** a moth irresistibly attracted to a candle (*taper*).

21 **die** here, as elsewhere in Donne, there may be a play upon *die*, meaning the loss of sexual power after consummation. The traditional idea that sexual intercourse shortens life may also be present.

22–7 The *eagle* is emblematic of masculine sexual initiative and the *dove* of female gentleness and sexual compliance. The *phoenix* is a mythical bird which every thousand years rejuvenates itself

59

by being consumed in flames and rising renewed from its ashes. It was thus emblematic of the resurrection, though here the renewal of sexual power – *we die and rise* (26) – is prominent.

27 **Mysterious**   does the poem makes us feel that their love is mysterious in the sense of being special and holy? In the following stanzas religious language enforces associations of other-worldliness, but does the impression that their love is only sexual athleticism still persist? Line 28 raises this problem acutely: if *die* is literal, then the religious language which follows might convince us that their love is truly mysterious, but what if the sexual connotations of *die* are acknowledged?

32 **sonnets... rooms**   *sonnets* here probably means love lyrics. In Italian, stanza, a unit of verse, means a room. This wordplay raises the question of whether at this point the speaker (or Donne?) is as interested in the nature of writing as in the nature of love. Consider, for instance, the force of *legend* (an inscription), *verse* and *hymns*.

38 **hermitage**   how far should this conceit be pressed? Does it signify their deep mutual understanding or does it point to their sexual union?

40–3 Do these lines mean that the lovers find in each other the essence of all that is valuable in the wider world, or that they possess each other so intensely that they seem to own everything?

45 **pattern**   this may recall the Platonic idea of Ideal Forms towards which the earthly world aspires. This raises the issue of whether the poet wants an earthly or a heavenly love.

The Damp

The voice of the poet is firm and purposeful, yet judging the poem's tone and attitude is no easy matter. Is, for instance, the opening scene of the autopsy anything more than grotesque comedy? And what is to be made of the frank language of the closing stanza with its playing on the sexual connotations of *die* (21). Is this an honest recognition of desire or a reductive picture of the relations between men and women?

Title   A *damp* is either a noxious fume or a moist, heavy air which depresses or even poisons those who breathe it.

1   **When I am dead**   the abrupt monosyllabic wording is echoed by other lines; for instance, *but if you dare be brave* (9). Does the monosyllabic thrust suggest annoyance, frustration, the desire to dominate or purposefulness?

3   **cut up**   a very emphatic stress falls upon these words. The words might bring out the oddity the poet feels at being an anatomical object or show hostility to the mistress.

4   **your picture in my heart**   is the tone here one of surprise similar to *The Relic* or perhaps grudging flattery, implying that her picture in his heart is only to be expected?

7   **prefer**   promote.

10   **pleasure**   the pleasure she takes in her conquests makes her a conventional cruel mistress, delighting in the sufferings she causes. It is, however, important to ask whether, in the poem as a whole, the poet thinks of his pleasure.

11   **enormous giant**   at this point the poem touches on the twilight world of medieval romance with its *enchantress* (12) and *witches* (18). This language works allegorically; the *enormous giant* is *your Disdain*. The implication might be that her morality is as out-dated as medieval literary forms. It may also be that Donne the poet enjoys working in another mode.

13   **Goth and Vandal**   the Goths and Vandals were Germanic tribes whose frequent and violent attacks brought about the downfall of the Roman Empire. Their names are traditionally associated with destruction.

16   **Kill... die**   see general note and *The Canonization* (21).

20–4   Do you recoil from the masculine assertiveness of these lines, particularly the demand that the woman exercise her *passive valour* (23)? Another possibility is that, as women were thought of as passive in the sexual act, *valour* (a term from medieval romance) might be a recognition of her power. But see note on line 11.

24   The idea is that in sexual encounters women can perform far longer than men.

The Dream

This poem's chief characteristic is the delight the poet takes in his extravagant wit. In the first eight lines, pleasure in his mistress leads him to that branch of philosophy called epistemology – the nature of and the methods used in gaining knowledge. His *dream* is a *theme/For reason* not *for phantasy* (3–4), and she is such as to *make dreams truths* (8). Plato is not very far away here. Later, there is a witty use of religious language. He implies that her knowledge is *beyond an angel's art* (16), thereby equating it with God's knowledge. Also bold is his use of *cam'st* (18), *rising* (22) and *goest to come* (29) as descriptive of the movements of the woman and the pattern of Christ's birth, rising from the dead, ascension into heaven and return at the end of time. Perhaps this is a poem that should just be enjoyed for the ease and ingenuity of Donne's art.

4 **phantasy**   fancy or make-believe rather than reality discovered through reason.

7 **true**   this may mean faithful and might also, in anticipation of 20, convey the idea that she is wonderfully *true* to herself.

9–10 Donne is interested in the movement from soul to body. Here, as in *The Ecstasy* (69), there is the issue of how fitting such a movement is. If the progression from *dreams* to *truths* and *fables* to *histories* (8) is a reasonable one, then might that from dreaming to acting also be natural?

16 **beyond an angel's art**   God, unlike angels, can read the thoughts of the heart. Readers might admire such a daring piece of wit, be surprised at the strangeness of the thought, recoil from its tastelessness, or be interested that he wants to use such language of his beloved.

22 **doubt**   fear.

26 **fear, shame, honour**   you might want to ask whether, from a woman's viewpoint, *fear* is justified, and *shame* inevitable once *honour* is lost.

27 **torches**   this is one of those moments when the reader might wonder how far to take this image. Is it a matter of *torches*

neatly balancing the earlier image of a *taper* (11)? And can
readers exclude the phallic associations of torches and candles?

30 **die**   what areas of meaning are involved here? Is it the
traditional association of sleep and death, or, even, the religious
associations discussed in the introduction to the poem? For the
sexual meaning see *The Canonization*, (21).

The Ecstasy

The Ecstasy resembles both some of the love and the religious
poems, except that it seems to lack the edgy ambivalence of the
former and the agonizing so often present in the latter.

    The poem is metaphysical in both literary and philosophical
senses. Conceits are drawn from several branches of learning
(literary sense), and it engages with such problems as the union of
souls and the relationship between soul and body (the
philosophical sense). In dealing with the union of souls, Donne
imaginatively fashions *soul's language* (22). Do we hear his pleasure
in the witty idea of *this dialogue of one* (74)? And perhaps, also,
readers, like the one who stands *Within convenient distance* (24),
might hear *soul's language* (22) in the music of the verse. The
gentle rhythms of reasonable argument, the conclusive cadences
at the close of the stanzas and delicate textures such as *But that it
first imprints the air* (58) might convince us that this is the refined
and elevated language that souls might use.

Title   An ecstasy is the temporary departure of the soul from the
body. The term, therefore, is not necessarily to be associated
with intense sensuous feelings.
In lines 1–28 the lovers sit on a bank, while their souls depart.
A lover is imagined as standing by. Lines 29–48 deal with what
the lover would hear the two souls say about the ecstatic state.
Lines 49–76 debate the return of the souls to their bodies.

1–4   This stanza raises a number of issues. Do *pillow* and *pregnant*
strongly suggest a sexual reading? The violet's *reclining head*
might suggest a posture of sexual compliance, though in

Donne's day the violet was an image of modesty and faithfulness. By contrast, the lovers modestly sit. Might *pregnant* merely refer to the shape of the bank?

4 **one another's best**   each is equally a wooer and a beloved.

5–6 **cemented/With a fast balm**   there are several possible meanings here: their hands are joined by their mutual sweat. *Balm* (sweat), according to a contemporary medical idea, keeps bodies from decay. Sweaty palms are a sign of sensuality.

7 **Our eye-beams twisted**   sight, it was believed, either came about because the eye transmitted a beam of light on to an object or received one emitted by an object. Their *eye-beams* twist because *thread* (7) and *string* (8) are made up of twisted fibres to give them strength.

10 **all our means**   what *means* would make them one? The words might either anticipate the union of souls or the union of bodies, discussed in 49–72.

11 **get**   beget. The word might look back to *pregnant* (2) and forward to *propagation* (12) and 37–40 about the transplanted violet. Is such language metaphoric or literal?

13 **Fate**   painters often represented *Fate* as poised above two opposing armies. As with every conceit, it is important to ask which implications of *Fate* and *two equal armies* are appropriate and whether other, perhaps less helpful, ones should be suppressed.

18 **We**   here the lovers are identified more fully with their bodies than their souls. Is this different from the use of *we* in line 51?
   sepulchral statues   statues on a funeral monument.

21 **refined**   made pure. The idea, derived from Alchemy, is also present in *concoction* (27).

25 **He**   why did Donne introduce someone who listens? Does he make the reader, who also listens, feel a member of a small and highly privileged group? Is there, perhaps, a hint of the love of display that is present in so many Donne poems?

31 **this**   ecstasy.

32 **what did move**   what motivated or moved us to act.

34 **Mixture**   it was believed that because the soul had so many functions, it was made up of a number of elements.

42 **Interinanimates**   a mutual infusion of life with a pun on *anima* (Latin for soul).

44 **loneliness** the state of being single.

   controls as in *The Good Morrow* Donne rhymes 'controls' with 'souls'. The rhyme could be no more than a useful coincidence of sounds or it could reveal Donne's interest in the relationship between love and power.

45 **know** might this word show that love is more a matter of knowledge than emotion? Think about whether love in *A Valediction: forbidding Mourning* is a matter of reason rather than passion.

47 **atomies** atoms.

48 **no change can invade** as the soul is eternal it cannot change. The military implications of *invade* raise the issue of whether metaphors and conceits should be restricted to their immediate setting or related to language elsewhere in the poem (see lines 13–17).

49 What kind of performance best suits this line: one that introduces a conscious element of theatricality or one that reads it as an expression of regret?

50 **forbear** avoid.

52 **intelligences... sphere** Aristotle taught that each heavenly body consists of a sphere governed and moved by a spirit or intelligence, which inhabits it.

55 **forces, sense** power of bodily movement, the five senses.

56 **dross... allay** dross is the waste product of an alchemical experiment: **allay** is an alloy which is a metal made by combining two or more metallic elements to give strength.

57–8 Donne might be referring to the idea that stars exert their influences by working through the air and/or the notion, present in *Air and Angels*, that angels can only influence people by appearing in bodies made out of the air.

62 **Spirits** this term was introduced to explain how the body related to the soul.

64 **subtle knot** the connection (*knot*) between body and soul is *subtle* in the sense that it is so elusive that it resists description and understanding.

65 **descend** Once more, there is the issue of how far to press Donne's language. Do *descend* and *reach* (67) suggest a model of mutual attraction and co-operation or, given that this is also the language of the Incarnation, are we also to suppose that the

relationship between body and soul and even the coupling of lovers can be compared to the birth of the Son of God?

68 Should the *prince* be interpreted as an imprisoned man or, as some have suggested, an unborn child in the womb?

69 It has been suggested that *The Ecstasy* is a poem of seduction. In favour is the fact that the needs of the body have been sounded since line 49, and at this point the poet makes a specific proposal. Against it is the point that nothing in the poem suggests that, in the sexual sense, they are not lovers already. Further, the return of the souls to the bodies does not necessarily mean they are going to make love. The meaning of the poem's last line has an important bearing on this question.

70 **Weak men** inferior lovers.

The Expiration

This was, in 1609, the first of Donne's poems to be printed. An appreciation of this beautiful poem depends upon the reader attending to its aching rhythms and the repetition of its soulful rhymes, which voice the traditional sound of lament – *So* (1), *owe* (5) and *Go* (6).

Title Three ideas are combined: the loss of breath in kissing, the breathing away of life at the moment of death and a substance being vaporized.

4 **happiest day** does this simply mean the happiest time of their life, or do the words point to how fleeting their time of love was?

11–12 Does *Except* introduce a clever afterthought which diverts the poet both from the sadness of the situation and his beloved, or does the emphatic alliteration of *double dead* convey an emotional flatness which shows the poet is devastated by the parting?

A Fever

In the opening and close the language of this poem is intimate and tender, whereas in the middle stanzas the writing is philosophically exact (read aloud the fourth stanza), and the beloved is spoken about rather than spoken to. What is to be made of this apparent disparity between feeling and thought? Perhaps the feeling is controlled by the subject matter – anguish at illness and philosophical notions about the end of the world. Perhaps, also, there is thought in the feeling and vice versa. And maybe the poet deliberately turns to argument as a diversion from the pain of the sick-bed. A complicating factor is the stanza form and the rhythms they create, which are ideally suited to the incisive expression of arguments. John Carey calls the rhythms *impudent*. They give the thought a tightly-packaged feel, which may be at odds not only with the emotion of the situation but also with the weighty topics such as death, the end of the world and the nature of the heavens.

1   **die… I**   does the internal rhyme enforce the pleading sigh of concern with which the poem opens or does it, by shifting attention to the poet, give the impression that his distress is greater than hers?

6–8   **this world**   in line 7 *this world* means the whole universe, whereas in line 8 it means her body. The linking of the microcosmic – the small world of her body – with the macrocosmic – the large world of the universe – is characteristic of metaphysical writing, though such intellectual ingenuity might be emotionally incompatible with the situation of a feverish girl and an anxious lover.

8   **vapours**   evaporates. Donne appears to be fascinated by evaporation. (See *The Expiration* (2), *Song: Sweetest love* (25–6) and *A Valediction: forbidding Mourning* (4).) This might be connected with his interest in time and death and / or with his preoccupation with what is material and immaterial, as in his treatment of body and soul.

12   **worms… worthiest**   does the alliteration diminish the world

without the beloved (men just become worthy *worms*) and so stress her importance, or is it a deviation from his concern for her into clever games with words?

13 **wrangling schools**   in the Middle Ages, groups (called schools) of philosophers debated exactly what kind of fire would burn at the end of the world.

19 **corruption**   contemporary medicine taught that fevers only last so long as there is corrupt or decaying matter in the body. The beloved is therefore an ideal figure, a virtuous beauty.

21–4 **meteors... firmament**   *meteors* soon burn themselves out because they are part of the changing world below the moon (see *A Valediction: forbidding Mourning*, line 13), whereas the *firmament* above is permanent, uncorrupted and therefore unchangeable.

25 **seizing**   physical holding and making a legal claim.

The Flea

The vivid presence of the poet, the way the reader is never allowed to forget the flea, and the remarkable way in which the mistress is present throughout, makes this one of Donne's most dramatically visual poems. But immediacy is only one of its pleasures; unlike some of Donne's poems, the argument does not meander but moves carefully, though easily, to its outrageous conclusion. As is often the case in Donne, the argument might be read as an actual attempt to persuade an unwilling woman to comply with the poet's desires, or as an intricate and enjoyable game, played with the woman or the reader or both. The way the crucial words *honour* (26) and *yield'st* (26) are significantly held back to the end of the poem might support the former view, though the skilful contrasts – innocence / guilt, death / life – strengthen the second interpretation. Those who interpret the poem as an attempt at seduction should consider the tone: is it pleading, cajoling, scheming, whining or patronizing? If the poem is a game to be enjoyed for itself, the poet / lover might be adopting the role of the mock preacher (*Mark but this flea* has the ring of a sermon about it) or the pseudo-scholar, who patiently explains a complex matter.

Title Poems about a lover envying the liberties a flea takes with his beloved's body were popular in sixteenth-century European poetry. Donne departs from convention by making the flea bite the lover as well as the woman and by presenting the lover as far more restrained than the flea, who *enjoys before it woo(s)* (7).

2 **that** is his reluctance to name what he desires part of a plan to make loss of virginity seem negligible, or is his evasiveness intended to stimulate her desire to yield on the grounds that that which is not named but strongly implied becomes alluring?

3 **Me... sucked... sucks... thee** does the *Me / thee* rhyme enforce the mutual character of the poem, or does the fact that *me* precedes *thee* point to a basic egocentricity? In *sucked*, Donne may have used the old fashioned form of 's', which resembles 'f'. If such a play (called an orthographic pun) is intended, should it be read as comically indecent, or does it tie in with the lover's strategy by feeding her, in a veiled form, the word which expresses his intention?

4 **mingled** a contemporary belief was that blood was *mingled* in sexual intercourse.

5 **Confess** the position and demanding tone of this word raises the question (a recurring one in Donne) of whether the poet wants to win the girl or the argument. The forceful monosyllables of the conclusion – *when thou yield'st to me* (26) – might suggest the former, but perhaps *this cannot be said* (5) and *Yet thou triumph'st, and say'st* (23) makes us think about how arguments are put into words.

8 **swells** how far should the connotations of this word be pressed beyond its primary meaning of the flea's body swelling with their blood? The suggestion of pregnancy (see the first stanza of *The Ecstasy*) would surely ruin the lover's strategy.

9 **alas** is this real feeling or a strategy of persuasion? A similar question can be asked of *'Tis true* (25).

10–11 A conceit upon the Holy Trinity. See, also, the note on line 18.

15 **cloistered** is the poet simply being comic by associating sexual union with the chaste life of the cloister, or should the

associations of seclusion and special religious status be taken to
indicate, as in *A Valediction: forbidding Mourning*, the self-
sufficiency of the world of love and the priesthood of lovers?
living walls of jet   this is a rare example of Donne writing
about nature (compare *Love's Growth*). *Jet* is a black semi-
precious stone (see *A Jet Ring Sent*).
16 **use**   her habit of denying him.
18 **sacrilege**   there may be a witty parallel between the flea, the
man and the woman, and the Holy Trinity of Father, Son and
Holy Ghost.
19 **Cruel and sudden**   the interpretation of the poem will be
evident in how these words are performed. The extent to which
the anger is assumed will have a bearing upon whether the
poem is a game or a serious exercise in wooing.

The Funeral

We must assume that the mistress has given the poet a lock of
her hair but has refused to give herself sexually. Does the poet
therefore sadly reflect on his lack of success or is he reproachful
or even spiteful? Another possibility is that he is fascinated by
the business of burial just as much as he is pained by his failure
in love. An interesting feature is the language level; on the one
hand the poet enjoys the exaggerated language of martyrdom
(dying for one's faith) and idolatry (worshipping idols), and on
the other there are very casual phrases such as *Whate'er she meant
by it* (17).

Title   The poem is about a funeral or, more specifically, the
preparation of the body for burial. In Donne's day most bodies
were buried in shrouds – tough canvas material wrapped round
the body and tied at the head and feet. There are some
similarities between this poem and *The Relic*, though the
occasion of the latter is not burial but the opening up of a
grave.
1 **harm**   one of the things this poem does is mysteriously

suggest that the hair is somehow alive. You might like to relate this to the discussion of the *sinewy thread* of his *brain* (9) and the tension, even paradox, of dead and living things.

2 **Nor question much**   is the effect that we do question?

3 **hair**   the mention of the lock of hair invites a comparison between this poem and *The Relic*.

6 **Viceroy**   one who acts in the place of an absent monarch. See *Holy Sonnet 14* (7).

which then to heaven being gone   is the poet concerned primarily with the grave, the hair and the woman, or does he speak lightly because he knows his soul will be safe in heaven?

7 **control**   a favourite word of Donne's, see *The Ecstasy* (44).

8 **her provinces**   does the admission that his body is subject to the rule of his mistress (a monarch might talk of ruling his or her provinces) flow naturally from the elevated and detailed way he has spoken of the lock of hair? You might feel it rudely interrupts the line of thought with the uncomfortable reminder that in spite of his persuasive power, the mistress is superior to him.

dissolution   consider the way the poem plays on the idea of corruption. He wishes to corrupt her by seduction, yet her hair preserves his body from the corruption of the grave (*dissolution*).

9–11 These lines depend upon a contemporary idea that the body was held together by sinews which ran from the brain.

14 **except**   unless.

19–20 For a discussion of martyrs and relics, see the notes on the titles of *The Canonization* and *The Relic*.

21–4 The reversal at the close is reminiscent of *Woman's Constancy*. Should the reversal be a complete surprise, or should some of the earlier lines be read in a tone of bitter irony so as to anticipate the poem's ending?

21 **humility**   subservience.

23 **bravery**   a defiant and rebellious gesture.

24 **bury**   the word may have sexual connotations.

The Good Morrow

This poem (an aubade or a poem set in the morning) makes the event of joyfully waking up with a loved one into an image of awakening into a new, adult life of love. This poem also uses the Renaissance imagery of voyages of exploration and map making. Does this imagery enforce the awakening to a new world of love or do the sea journeys serve as a contrast to the lovers' inner (and more authentic) renaissance?

2 **we**   compare the transformation of *thou* and *I* into *we* with the way in which *me* and *thee* becomes *our* in *The Flea*. Are there significant differences in tone between these grammatical changes?

3 **sucked on country pleasures, childishly**   affluent citizens sent their children into the country to be breast-fed by wet nurses. The possible sexual connotations, such as the pun on *country*, might indicate that in their 'childish' state their love was merely physical. See the note on *The Flea* (3).

4 **seven sleepers**   a legend records that seven Christian youths, who were sealed alive in a cave during persecution by the Emperor Decius, slept for 187 years till they were awakened.

5 **but this**   compared to this.

10 **controls**   does this word betray a desire in the speaker (in Donne?) to dominate, or could it be a simple acknowledgement that love is so powerful that it can control love of lesser things? Donne displays a characteristic verbal dexterity in the witty idea of love controlling love.

13–14 The sense of the argument is: what does it matter even though... .

15 **appears**   the placing of this word at the end of the line acts out the joyful recognition that each person's face is seen reflected in the other. Should we ignore the suggestion of falseness, of appearance rather than reality?

18 **sharp north... declining west**   north is a traditional symbol of coldness and *west* of things in decline. Can the sexual connotations that she will not be cold and his powers will not decline be excluded?

19 According to medieval and Renaissance medicine, death occurs when the elements that make up living things are unequally mixed.

21 **slacken... die** should the possible sexual undertones of *slacken* (lose vigour) and *die* (loss of sexual power after sexual consummation) be acknowledged? If they are, do they diminish the poem by suggesting that love is merely sexual activity or enrich it through the recognition that sexuality has an important role? A similar issue is encountered in *The Canonization*.

A Jet Ring Sent

This poem is untypical of Donne in that it accepts the conventional attitude of a lover complaining about the cruelty of his mistress. Nor is there much sense of intellectual adventure; the poet does not use himself, his mistress nor the ring as starting-points for ingenious speculations. Do you find it narrow and disappointing or do you enjoy its direct, no-nonsense tone, as heard in *Marriage rings are not of this stuff* (5)?

Title Jet rings were fashionable and quite cheap. They were often lined with silver and because they could be inscribed they became popular as love tokens. There is some contemporary evidence that they were worn on the thumb.

1 **Thou** the poet frequently addresses the ring as *thou* or *thee*. Is it more consistently present to him than is the beloved in some of the other poems? Could it be that the poet addresses his mistress through the ring because that way he finds it easier to maintain a steady emotional engagement?
black a symbol of constancy, because there are no tonal variations in black.

2 **brittle** inconstant, frail and unserious.

3 **spoke** symbolized. See *Figure* (7).

5 **Marriage rings** these are usually made of gold and so, unlike jet rings, are *precious* (6) and *tough* (6).

7–8 Is the poet artistically pleased with the way the ring so perfectly represents (*Figure*) both their loves, or does he regretfully imply

that he wishes it were not such an intellectually and
emotionally appropriate image?

8 **Except** unless.

8–9 **fling me away... Yet stay** as well as the contrast between *fling*
and *stay* there is probably a pun on *jet* which, by derivation
from the French *jette* (to throw), was a medieval word meaning
to throw or cast away.
Do you think the contrast is too neat and calculated or does it
reveal tenderness in the poet, who, because he has been hurt, is
sensitive to others – even rings?

12 **oh** this could be a conventional poetic way of indicating
feeling or it could mark a change from subdued or muted grief
to uncontrolled anguish.

Lovers' Infiniteness

The emotional tone of this poem is, at times, that of a puzzled
and perhaps even vulnerable man, who is anxious about whether
his mistress entirely loves him. The poem's argument, however,
has a strict mathematical and legalistic character. Is there a
tension between feeling and thought? Another feature is that the
poem is smoother than those in which harsh rhythms express a
forthright speaking voice.

Title Is the infinity that of love itself or the lovers? There is a 1612
setting of a version of this poem by the composer John Dowland.

1 When reading this line aloud you will have to do justice both
to the reasoned character of *If* and the (sad? puzzled?
despairing?) emotional lilt of the words.
all the poem's central word: 2, 5, 11, 12, 13 (twice), 22, 23,
24, 33. But is it always used with the same shade of meaning
and the same emotional weight?

3–4 In love poetry, particularly of the Petrarchan kind, lovers sigh
and weep. It is important to ask whether Donne accepts the
convention or whether there is a degree of ironic undermining.

5 **treasure... purchase** the idea of wealth which can be
measured out becomes one of the controlling images of the

poem. Does he intend the poem to work by playing off the image of love as measurable against the common belief that it cannot be measured? You might also ask whether the idea of measuring love is present in the use of *all*?

8 **bargain** although this word might seem gross and cold-blooded, it was used by Elizabethan love poets. For instance, Sir Philip Sidney's *My true love hath my heart and I have his* has this line: *There never was a better bargain driven*.

9 **gift** this word and *gavest* (12) apparently contradict words such as *treasure* (5), *purchase* (5) and *spent* (6). Is this a way of establishing a tension between two ideas of love, or could it be that men pay whereas women give?

16 **stocks** is this meant to contrast unfavourably with the word that applies to his capacity for love – *treasure* (5)?

18 **fears** anxieties and doubts. It is worth asking of this and other poems, how safe the lovers in Donne's poem feel.

21 **ground** in law the crops that grow from a patch of purchased land belong to the new owner.

23 Having said he wanted all her love, he now says he does not want it yet. This is a good place to think about the role of anticipation in both Donne's love and religious poetry. How often do the poems look forward to something rather than celebrate its occurrence in the past or present?

32 **changing hearts** if this is an echo of the Sir Philip Sidney poem quoted above (8), then the poet may be proposing marriage. This would be consistent with *so we shall/Be one*. But as *liberal* could mean speaking openly about sexual matters, he might only be suggesting sexual intercourse.

Love's Alchemy

An angry poem, but at whom or what is the anger directed? The insulting coarseness of *centric happiness* (2) and the dismissive closing couplet might suggest it is a woman or women in general. But it might be love itself, because it has not brought him the joys commonly associated with it (see lines 11–12 on the brevity of sexual pleasure). A third possibility is that it is the elevated language used by poets and lovers. The poem opens with a challenge to speech; those who claim to experience the depths of love should *Say* where it lies. And what is the actual tone of the anger: is it cynical, bitter, disappointed, resentful, envious or even enjoyably self-dramatizing? In thinking over this issue, you need to take account of the poem's abrupt rhythms and abrasive sound textures.

Title Alchemy was a highly complex study, one of the aims of which was to discover, by quasi-chemical means, the philosopher's stone, which would change ordinary metals into gold. As this stone was thought to bestow the power of preservation upon those who possessed it, the title is appropriate: the poet regrets that sexual pleasure is so brief and looks to Alchemy to prolong it.

1–2 *deeper digged love's mine* and *centric happiness* may be crude sexual joking. As a variation of this interpretation, it could be that the poet is using economic exploitation as an analogy of men's sexual enterprises.

3–4 The verbs could express the pride of the sexual athlete and so make the reader recognize him as a man of experience, or they could reduce him to a list of bodily movements carried out in rapid succession in an impersonal and mechanical way.

6 **imposture** a bogus claim.

7 **chemic** alchemist.

8 **pregnant pot** alchemical cauldron in which experiments are prepared.

10 **odoriferous thing, or medicinal** marginally useful by-products of alchemical experiments.

13 **our** the change from singular to plural could indicate that the poet is consoling himself by recognizing that he is one of a band of many lovers, or that he has in mind the smaller group, who see through the silly claims of idealistic lovers.

18 **loving wretch** is the loving wretch a lover or a love poet? Given that the poem is a palinode (a poem that contradicts something written in an earlier poem), could it be that Donne is criticizing something that he himself has said in an earlier poem? If so, which poem, or poems, might he have in mind?

22 **spheres**   the music made by the revolution of the heavens.

23–24   the poet could be saying that, even at their most attractive,
women are possessed by demons, or that even the most
engaging women are of no more interest or value than dead
flesh (*mummy*) once they have been sexually *possessed*.

Love's Growth

As is common in Donne, the astonishing experience of love
leads to a philosophical meditation, which is expressed in
conceits, drawn from Alchemy, Astronomy and Medicine.
Another philosophical element is the traditional conflict
between fixed, changeless ideas of perfection and the fact of
growth and change. The different modes of speech – intellectual
exactitude (7–14), nonchalant observation (11–12) and intimate
address, as in line 24, are testing for a performer. Also testing is
whether the poem should be delivered as an address to a beloved,
a speech to love itself, or a musing soliloquy from which the
poet momentarily awakens in 24?

1 **pure**   in Alchemy a substance was *pure* when it was simple and
unchangeable.

3 **endure**   undergo.

4 **Vicissitude**   change, alteration.

grass   grass is a traditional symbol of the decay to which all
natural things are subject – 'The days of man are as grass, as a
flower of the field, so he flourisheth. For the wind goeth over
it, and it is gone' (Psalm 103:15–16). Is decay as opposed to
growth present anywhere else in the poem, and is its presence
or its absence significant?

In 4 the poet has made the discovery (a disturbing or joyful
one?) that love is not unchanging but, in the words of the
poem, *elemented* (13); that is, part of the changing world of
Nature. Compare the idea of love growing with the claim that it
is unchanging in *The Anniversary* and *The Good Morrow*.

6 **more**   an important word in the poem (8, 15).

8 **quintessence** contemporary belief held that all things were made of the four elements: earth, air, fire and water. Some thinkers speculated that there was a fifth element, *quintessence*, which cured all ills, hence line 7.

9 **paining** this could mean causing pain or having an influence upon soul, or sense.

10 **working** it was believed that the sun produced warmth, growth and (by implication) a renewal of sexual energy. See also (25).

11–12 These lines are clearly directed at poets (the *Muse* is the source of poetic inspiration). Is there an uneasy relationship between this and other poems by Donne? *The Undertaking*, for instance, sees love as pure and abstract.

14 **do** might the strong implication of sexual activity exclude other meanings of the word *love*?

19–20 Does the rare use of natural imagery make vivid the beauty of a changing love, or is the reader inevitably reminded, as in *grass* (4), of how short life and love can be?

20 **awakened root** the phallic implications raise the same question as *do* (14).

23 **spheres** the heavens were thought of as a set of spheres, all of which had their centre in the earth – hence *concentric* (24).

A Nocturnal upon S. Lucy's Day, being the shortest day

The reader who wants to appreciate what this poem is saying about loss, grief and feelings of nothingness and negativity should attend to its rhythms and sounds. Crucial to the whole argument of the poem is the phrase *But I am none* (37), which is the start of the last, and possibly most buoyant, stanza, and yet, as a cadence, it is flat and even inert. The co-existence of negatives – *privations* (16), *things which are not* (18) – with the much repeated word *all* raises the question of whether, as a whole, the poem is dark and negative or strangely positive in spite of its subject matter.

Title   Until the calendar was altered in 1752, St Lucy's Day (13 December) was the shortest of the year. The choice of day has prompted speculation that Donne wrote the poem for Lucy, Countess of Bedford, either during a severe illness which she suffered in the winter of 1612 / 13 or after her death in 1627. The dead beloved might also be Donne's wife, Ann, who died in 1617. There is, however, no reason why an actual event must have prompted the poem.

3 **flasks**   the stars were thought to store up light originally given out by the sun and so could metaphorically be spoken of as the *flasks* – powder-flasks – in which gunpowder was kept.

4 **light squibs**   the brief flashes and small explosions of a firework.
    constant   this clearly contrasts with the brief flashes of the *squibs*, but applied to the bereft lover it might mean that without his beloved it is hard to be *constant*.

6 **general balm**   either another term for *The world's whole sap* (5) or the preserving substance which, according to some contemporary medical views, prevented decay. *Balm* also soothes and heals.
    hydroptic earth   the earth, like someone suffering from the disease of dropsy, is full of water and yet insatiably thirsty. It is interesting to speculate why Donne employs this image. See *Elegy* 4 (6) and *Holy sonnet 17*.

7 **bed's-feet**   it was believed that life ebbs away from a dying

man towards his feet; it could also mean that a dying man's life – his interests and concerns – shrinks to the dimensions of the bed upon which he lies.

10 **Study me then** this raises the familiar problem of sincerity or showiness: is he uncomfortably aware of his extreme condition, or making a self-centred theatrical gesture?

11 What is the effect of the pace of this line and the positioning of *next world* and *spring*? You might read it as a piece of poetic exaggeration or feel that spring, and all it stands for, really is a long way off.

13 **alchemy** alchemy searched for the elixir of life – the essence of life, which cured all ills. Here, however, love produces in him the elixir of death and negativity.

17 The words *ruined* and *re-begot* may allude to the fall of mankind and the salvation, or new birth, brought about by Christ. Are these ideas important in the poem?

21 **limbeck** apparatus used in Alchemy to distil (*draw*) substances.

22–7 These lines are apparently in the fashionable Petrarchan mode; that is, they indulge in dramatic exaggeration such as the tears of lovers drowning the world. There might also be Biblical overtones of Creation and Flood. If so, what is their contribution?

28 The fact that *death* is qualified by the remark that the *word wrongs her* indicates that at this point the poem is concerned with the adequacy of words to their subject matter. Are there are other moments when the subject of the poem becomes the poet's difficulty of expressing exactly what he is feeling? This question can, of course, be asked of other poems.

29 **first nothing** the state of the world before creation may be hinted at here, because Christian doctrine insists that the world was made out of *nothing*.
   elixir see note on *alchemy* (13).

31 **prefer** choose.

33 **Some ends, some means** aims or goals (*ends*), and the ways of achieving them (*means*).

34 **some properties invest** all things that exist have distinguishing characteristics.

37 **nor will my sun renew** is he saying that his spiritual winter is so deep that he can expect no spring – no revival of his spirits – or

that the sun, the light of life, is identified with his dead beloved?

38 **lesser sun** the real sun.

39 **Goat** the sign of Capricorn which, according to the old Calendar, the sun enters on 12 December. The goat is traditionally associated with *lust* (40).

41 This line is very much a case of how performance affects interpretation. Should it be read self-pityingly, enviously or in a spirit of generous recognition of others' good fortune?

42 **festival** this word introduces a sustained conceit based upon religious ritual – *prepare* (43), *hour* (44), *vigil* (44), *eve* (44). The poet could be commemorating her and thinking upon himself at the darkest time of the year, or preparing himself to meet her in death.

45 **is** a paradox of this poem is that though it is built on negatives it ends with *is*.

The Relic

There are two interesting tensions in this poem. The first is the very strong contrast between the poem's opening with its graphic preoccupation with graves and bones and the completely spiritual love celebrated at the close. The second is the familiar one in Donne of elevated claims about love and the poem's light movement, diverting asides and flippant dismissals. *The Relic* resembles *The Canonization* in that the lovers become objects of religious devotion, and the large claims advanced through the central conceits are ingeniously shown to be appropriate to the earthly love the couples enjoy.

Title Relics are the bones or belongings of saints, the veneration (honouring) of which was an important aspect of medieval Catholicism. The Thirty-nine Articles, which set out doctrine for the Church of England, said that the 'Worshipping and Adoration of relics is a fond (foolish) thing, vainly invented, and grounded upon no warranty of Scripture, but rather repugnant to the Word of God.' As with the religious poems, it is interesting to ask whether Donne still thinks as a Catholic or whether he adopts the official Anglican point of view. The word *mis-devotion* (13) suggests the poem is Anglican, but the imagery might show that his imagination is still Catholic.

1–2 It was a common practice to bury bodies in old graves.
broke this word could serve as a foil to the surprising note of courtesy in the second line, or its harshness might indicate the resentment lovers feel at being disturbed in their happy isolation. See *alone* (7).

3 **woman-head** the primary meaning is the way women behave, but there might also be a play on maidenhead.

5 **spies** does the poet resent being spied upon, or is there a barely concealed delight in being seen? This issue is also present in *The Canonization* and *The Sun Rising*.

6 **bracelet of bright hair** a love token of fair hair. Since her hair is the only part of her in the grave, it is surprising that the poet speaks so confidently about a loving couple (8).

10–11 **the last busy day** the Day of Judgement when, in Christian belief, at the second coming of Christ, bodies arise from their graves to be re-joined with their souls (see *Holy Sonnet 7*). Does the language used here devalue the idea of the Last Judgement by reducing it to a busy day, or does it reveal a touching desire on the part of the poet that, even at the climax of world history, there should be time for lovers to meet?

12 **fall** occur.

16 **to make** In the light of the prosaic *he that digs us up* (14), the transformation of the lovers into saints might appear ludicrous, but, given that it is Donne's idea that the *Bishop and the King* pronounce them saints, could it be that he enjoys, and thereby endorses, this promotion to sainthood?

17 **Mary Magdalen** St Mary Magdalen was a follower of Jesus who, in the imagination of the Church, has become identified with the prostitute, who, in St Luke's Gospel, washes Jesus's feet and dries them with her hair. She is usually portrayed as having long, flowing hair.

18 Might the poet be identified with Christ? There was certainly one tradition that Christ and Mary Magdalen were in love. Christopher Ricks observed that Jesus Christ has the same syllabic count as *something else*. But there are alternatives. He

could be regarded as another saint or, jokingly, as one of Mary Magdalen's lovers – a very unlikely candidate for sainthood. Above all, the difficulty is that in the New Testament Christ's tomb is empty, so there would be no bones in it. It may be that the problem should be looked at from another angle: could it be that the poet jokingly mocks the age of *mis-devotion* for mistaking him for Christ and for thinking that his chaste beloved might be a prostitute?

19 **and some men**   the joke is that women are supposed to be more superstitious than men.

21 **paper**   poem.

22 **miracles**   relics of saints were believed to bring about miracles.

25–6 The belief referred to here is that each person is watched over by his or her own guardian angel. Angels were commonly believed to have no sexual characteristics.

27–8 A kiss of greeting and a kiss when parting was a common practice that implied no sexual interest between people.

29–30 Where does the poem stand over the matter of chastity? The miracle could be that the two overcame the temptation to touch *the seals* (sexual organs). Another possibility is that *injured* might imply that *late law* has done nature wrong, and that, therefore, the poet is regretting intercourse is prohibited.

32 **pass**   surpass.

Song: Go, and catch a falling star

It is hard to disagree with Coleridge's judgement (found in his notebooks) of this vigorous and forthright poem: 'Life from crown to sole'. The poet takes pleasure in his own gusto. In the poem's restless rhythms and its pose of disengaged cynicism, we might hear the poet enjoying the absurdity that a woman could be both beautiful and faithful. But perhaps the possibility of there being such a woman gives the poem life.

1–9 Listing impossible activities was a feature of contemporary love poetry. Donne might be mocking the absurdity of this convention by asserting that *a woman true, and fair* (18) does not exist. Though it might be that he playfully relishes the prospect of such fantastic exploits.

1 **Go** is this addressed to a would-be lover who believes in female fidelity, a fellow poet or an adventurer who seeks wonders?

falling star since falling star(s) – shooting stars – were thought to be signs of impending disaster, it could be that the impossibility the poet has in mind is controlling fate.

2 **mandrake root** the idea of making a mandrake root, which resembled the human shape, pregnant is absurd in at least two ways: legend has it that when pulled up its scream kills those who hear it, and, in some cases, it resembles the male and not the female form.

4 **the Devil's foot** the devil is commonly represented as having a cloven hoof. To ask who *cleft* it is to engage in an occult version of the highly speculative questions that fascinated medieval theologians, and, in some poems, Donne.

5 **mermaids** mermaids, or sirens, were thought to lure sailors on to rocks by their beautiful singing. The line may reveal heroic ambitions: does he want to be like the Greek hero, Odysseus, who, because be was tied to a mast, heard the sirens yet survived?

8 **wind** a favourable wind for sailors.

9 **honest** this could refer specifically to a true and faithful lover or, more generally, to the honest person who has no hope of advancement in a corrupt world.

10 **be'est born to** have an inclination to.

strange sights neither here nor in *strange wonders* (15) is there an attempt to convey the feel of strangeness or wonder. Perhaps wonder is impossible because there are no *strange sights*. Perhaps the poet is concealing his disappointment.

11 **Things invisible to see** the reading of this crucial line affects the interpretation of the poem. Does the poet play with an oxymoron (a verbal contradiction) or is he drawn to the paradox of being able to see that which is invisible? Compare *The Undertaking* 17–20.

18 **true, and fair** is the poem weakened because it

unquestioningly accepts this (typically male) idea? Perhaps,
however, in the cadence of *true, and fair* there is the momentary
and joyful glimpse that such a person may exist.

20 **pilgrimage... sweet** in contemporary literature lovers were
often spoken of as pilgrims. Again, does this word, albeit
momentarily, suggest the possibility that there actually is a
woman *true, and fair*? If so *sweet* should be read without irony.

22 **next door** consider the effect of this familiar, domestic term
in a poem about heroic tasks and *All strange wonders* (15). Is it
cynicism – he will not even go next door to see a woman who
might be *true, and fair* – or cheerful resignation to a world
without such *wonders*?

27 **ere I come** what does he want of the woman who might be
true, and fair? Would he admire or court her?

two, or three does this reveal regret or dismissive cynicism?

Song: Sweetest love, I do not go

This poem is uncharacteristic of Donne in that there is little
philosophizing, and the rhythms of the verse, unlike, for instance,
Song: Go, and catch a falling star, are smooth and mellifluous.
What it does share with other poems is a preoccupation with
parting, an anxiety about time and the problem of whether the
poet consistently tries to comfort his beloved or becomes
distracted by his own ideas.

Title In his *Life of Donne*, Isaac Walton claims that this poem, along
with *A Valediction: forbidding Mourning*, was written in 1611
shortly before Donne parted from his wife to travel on the
Continent.

4 **fitter** is this a compliment or, given *me* at the end of the line,
concealed egotism?

8 **feigned deaths** is this moving because it is an ineffectual joke
offered in the hope of cheering up his beloved, or is there the
uncomfortable implication that if his deaths are *feigned*, his
grief at parting may also be fake?

11 The sun has neither will (*desire*) nor awareness (*sense*).

13–14 **fear not me/But believe**   perhaps an echo of *Fear not, believe only*, St Luke 8:50.

16 **wings and spurs**   he could be casting himself in the role of Mercury – the winged messenger of the Greek and Roman gods.

17 **feeble**   this marks a decisive change of tone. It could make the poem seem inconsistent or could be read as a deliberate restraint after the poetic flights of fancy in the second stanza.

19 **Cannot add**   perhaps an echo of St Matthew 6: 27: *Which of you by taking care, is able to add one cubit unto his stature?* Coleridge praised this poem for its religious thoughtfulness and faith, possibly because of its awareness, both here and in 17, of human limitation.

21–4   Consider how the structure of the stanza makes these lines different in their effectiveness and significance from the preceding four lines. This question may also be asked of other stanzas in the poem.

23 **teach it art and length**   give it cunning (*art*) and allow it scope (*length*).

25–32   When reading this poem aloud, particular attention must be given to bringing out the significance of the assonance on 'i'. Elsewhere in the poem, the long and short 'e' sounds help to establish the tone.

26 **sigh'st my soul away**   sighing was believed to shorten life.

27 **unkindly kind**   should this phrase (an oxymoron or verbal contradiction) be seen as a clever phrase offered by the poet to cheer up his beloved or does its very ingenuity weaken the point that although her tears are natural (*kind*) they might harm him (*unkindly*)?

32 **the best of me**   my very self.

33 **divining**   foreseeing the future.

34 **Forethink**   Donne quite often forethinks – speaks with assurance about what will happen in the future.

36 **fears**   are they just her fears?

38 **turned aside to sleep**   compare this with the closing three stanzas of *A Valediction: forbidding Mourning*. Do you think a poem about parting is more effective when it uses familiar, domestic details such as the couple turning aside from each other to sleep, or does the strange appropriateness of the

compasses conceit get closer to the idea that though apart they are not really parted?

The Sun Rising

This poem opens like *The Canonization* with an outburst against an intruder upon the intimate world of the lovers and it closes (as does *The Relic*) by establishing a link between the world of their love and the world at large. Yet there are features that make this poem quite distinctive. One such feature is the masculine, possessive pride the lover takes in his beloved. Coleridge responded to this aspect when he wrote: 'Fine, vigorous exaltation, both soul and body in full puissance'. In the full joy of possessing his beloved, he extravagantly claims that their love is so intensely real that it constitutes the basic reality of the world, even to the point of saying *Nothing else is* (22). Perhaps the strength of the poem is that he almost compels us to agree with him.

Title Like *The Good Morrow* this is an aubade, a song sung in the morning.

1   Does the poet adopt the role of the young rebel deriding the older and feebler generation, or might he be anticipating stanza three by speaking in an authoritative and even kingly tone?

3   **curtains**   probably those round a four-poster bed rather than at the windows.

5–8   Are these lines contemptuously dismissive of people whose activities are banal, or do they show that he finds them interesting, purposeful and attractive?

5   **saucy**   impertinent with possibly a hint of lechery.
    pedantic   in the manner of a schoolmaster.

7   **court-huntsmen**   members of the court who hunt or self-seekers who hunt for a position or promotion at court. Both senses could be combined: James I was fond of early morning hunting, so those wishing to curry favour would be up early to join him.

8   **country ants to harvest offices**   this probably means hardworking farmers, engaged in harvesting.

9–10 These lines explore the tension between praise of a permanent, unchanging state and a fascination with the variety of the physical world, which is subject to time and change. Does the elevated tone and the measured, majestic pace convince you that an eternal and unchanging state is both superior and desirable, or does the vividness of *rags of time* direct you to the keen pleasures, albeit fleeting ones, that are to be found in the world? This tension is central to Donne's poetry.

9 **Love, all alike**   love which never changes.

13 **wink**   the basic meaning in the seventeenth century was a closing of the eye, though the meaning of a discreet and knowing signal was also available.

14 **her sight**   sight of her.

15 **eyes**   poets conventionally wrote of the brightness of their beloved's eyes and frequently compared them to the sun.

17 The East Indies produced spices, and the West Indies were mined for gold. The images could suggest her alluring richness, or the poet might regard his beloved as an object to be exploited.

20 **hear... here**   perhaps the playfulness of the echo indicates the intellectual superiority of the poet over the sun?

21 The swelling movement of this line might express the lover's (understandable) possessive pride in such a beautiful woman. Might it also reveal his desire to control and dominate?

22 **Nothing else is**   in the light of the introductory remarks, perhaps we should ponder whether these emphatic words really insist that the love the couple share is the only fundamental reality.

23 **play**   does this word raise the issue of who is doing the playing? A similar question is raised by *mimic* (24).

24 **alchemy**   dazzling but superficial.

25 **half**   since the sun is single he can only be half as happy as the couple.

29 **Shine**   the order to *shine* on the lovers is a dramatic change from the opening, where the sun's intrusion was resented. Is there a progression from anger to acceptance?

30 **centre... sphere**   Donne employs a geocentric rather than a heliocentric picture of the world. We might say that though it is not scientifically correct, it is still our everyday experience that the sun does indeed appear to move around the earth.

The Triple Fool

In some respects this is a light poem: it is humorously directed against the poet himself, several of its lines are short, and some of the rhyming couplets could even be described as snappy. Yet it gives a quite detailed consideration of important matters: how the discipline of art (in this case poetry) controls personal feeling, and how art in performance can awaken in a listener the feelings that inspired the artist. To put it another way: the writer is lover, poet and listener.

Title The occasion is a musical performance of one of the writer's poems. The title invites us to ask in what ways the poet is a triple fool.

4 **wiseman** not only someone who is wise but also the person who appears wise in the ways of the world.

5 **deny** is this weak self-justification or is it a much tougher and more knowing recognition that if he were successful in love, even the *wiseman* would envy him?

6–7 The popular belief was that sea water is salty but land water fresh, because land water had passed through subterranean passages in which it lost its saltiness. The language conveys a very strong sense of the inner life of the poet, suggesting through the image of *earth's inward narrow crooked lanes* the secret depths of the self and the mysterious processes that occur in the mind.

10 **numbers** a common term for poetry.

22 You may feel that the ending is good because it takes up the theme of wise men and fools or that its proverb-like quality is out of keeping with the narrative character of the poem.

Twicknam Garden

This zestful poem enjoyably plays with the renaissance conventions of the distraught lover / poet. There is a dramatic mismatch between the seasons and mood of the poet, and his weeping appears to be perpetual. It is difficult to tell whether the pain of an unrequited lover can be felt in and through the self-conscious display of the poetic persona.

Title Twicknam Park was the home from 1607 of Donne's patroness, Lucy, Countess of Bedford. The garden was elaborately laid out on a symmetrical plan, which represented the geocentric image of the universe. Lucy's garden did not contain fountains, but Donne might have been familiar with them from other formal gardens.

1–5 The changing rhythms of these lines could mark the depth of his anguish, or indicate an element of self-parody.

2 **spring** in poetry moods are frequently compared and contrasted with the seasons.

4 **balms** medicinal preparations which soothe and heal. Donne also alludes to extreme unction – the annointing of the eyes before death.

6 **spider love** it was believed that a spider changed everything it ate into poison.
transubstantiates the Roman Catholic Church taught that Christ's presence in the Mass was brought about by a change in the substance of the bread, so that although it looked unchanged its real nature had been transformed. This doctrine was called transubstantiation.

7 **manna to gall** the children of Israel were fed in the desert by the miraculous appearance of a bread-like food called *manna*. Hence in Christian symbolism *manna* is a foreshadowing and sign of the holy communion or mass. *Gall* is a sharp-tasting herb which throughout the Bible symbolizes bitter experience.
      Converting *manna to gall* is a reversal of the action of the mass and might also be a subversion of the poetic convention that love is a religion.

9 **True paradise... the serpent** according to the book of Genesis in the Bible, Adam and Eve were expelled from the Garden of Eden, or paradise, because they yielded to the serpent's temptation.

10 **wholesomer** better in the sense of more fitting and more appropriate.

11 **Benight** overcome with darkness.

15 **nor yet leave loving** what is to be made of the poet's desire
to continue loving and yet avoid its pain (*senseless* means
without sensation)? Does it successfully show a man in the
paradoxical state of hating the pain of love yet longing to
continue loving? Perhaps it shows a liking for strange and
extreme states.

17 **mandrake** a plant which was supposed to scream when
uprooted. See *Song: Go, and catch a falling star* (2).

19–25 What is the relationship between the poet's emotions and the
imagery? Are his feelings momentarily allayed by the ingenuity
of the fountain image before they break out in *Alas, hearts...* ,
or is that outburst as staged as the image (a comic one?) of
lovers tasting their mistress's tears?

19 **vials** tear-vessels.

20 **love's wine** possibly a reference to wine consecrated in the mass.

27–8 The close of the poem might be an anguished image of the
poet's misfortune in loving a woman who, unlike all others, is
faithful to someone else. There might also be a hint of comedy
in the absurd situation of loving the one woman who will
remain faithful.

The Undertaking

There is a puzzling tension between the elevated subject and the
poem's form and tone. The poem celebrates *loveliness within* (13),
and yet the metre is brisk, and the tone proud, boasting and
perhaps even smugly self-satisfied. A further aspect of this tension
is that between the refined character of the love and the terse,
philosophical force of the argument. These disparities were noted
by Coleridge, who wrote: 'A grand poem; and yet the tone, the
riddle character, is painfully below the dignity of the main thought'.

Title An alternative title is *Platonic Love*. Platonism taught that what
is visible is only a dim reflection of the real world, which exists
in an eternal and unchangeable form. For Platonists, it follows
that the highest kind of love ignores the body and seeks only
the mind, because it is more akin to the eternal and unchanging

world. The contrast between the material world and the real world is present in a number of Donne's poems.

1 **braver** finer, more glorious and more impressive.

2 **Worthies** the *Worthies* were nine heroic figures who exemplified all the qualities of ideal warriors. In public pageants they were represented by men, who loudly boasted about the *Worthies'* marvellous deeds.

4 **hid** it is unusual to find a poem celebrating secrecy when so many of Donne's poems are showy and theatrical. Does the poet keep his secret hidden?

6 **specular stone** a transparent stone used in building ancient temples. Since Donne and his contemporaries believed that it was no longer available, there was no point in learning the very difficult art of cutting it.

8 **cut** a reader must do justice to the particularly incisive stress on this word.

14/16 **loathes / oldest clothes** do you think the poet finds it easy to dismiss colour and skin as *clothes*, which are to be loathed? You might also ask whether the insistence of the rhyme creates the impression that *inner loveliness* matters more than the flesh.

17 **as I have** see *Twicknam Garden* (19–22) for another view of the poet as a pattern of true love.

18 **Virtue attired** if you have decided that *oldest clothes* make the flesh faded and uninteresting, is it possible to respond positively to the image of *Virtue* clothed in a *woman*?

19 **say** does the poet's real achievement lie not in loving but in saying?

20 **the He and She** as the sentence starts with a questioning *If* (17), is there a hint that the poet acknowledges that it is very difficult to ignore sexuality?

22 **profane men** poets often spoke of love as a religion and of ordinary lovers as irreligious or *profane*. See also the second stanza of *A Valediction: forbidding Mourning*.

A Valediction: forbidding Mourning

The relationship between reason and emotion in this poem is particularly enigmatic: is it an argument touched by emotion, or a lovingly intimate poem that controls feeling by expressing it in the form of an argument?

Title A valediction is a poem of farewell. If Isaac Walton is right in saying that this poem was written by Donne when he parted from his wife for a journey to France in 1611, the *I* of the poem may be the poet himself. If, however, this is a guess, both the *I* and *thou* could be fictional. Would this make a difference?

As this word often introduces an argument: might it also introduce a more emotional kind of speech?

virtuous men those with a clear conscience die peacefully.

5 **melt** think about the force of this word in the light of its common meaning in Donne's day of yielding to an emotion or giving way to tears. Consider, also, its importance in the poem in relation to the plea for *firmness* (35).

11 **trepidation** the system of astronomy originated by Ptolemy held that the spheres surrounding the earth trembled (*trepidation*) as they revolved; this affected the motion of the planets but was neither felt nor caused damage on earth. It was, thus, *innocent* (12); that is to say, harmless.

13 **Dull sublunary lovers** since the Fall ruined the region below the moon, earthly lovers are tarnished.

14 **(Whose soul is sense)** *sublunary lovers* are *dull* because their affections originate from, and are entirely controlled by, the senses.

17 **refined** purified.

20 **Care less** what force do these words have, given that the poet lingers over *eyes, lips, and hands* before coming to the word *miss*?

24 **aery thinness beat** gold beaten to a near transparent state to produce gold leaf.

25–36 In Donne's day compasses performed the tasks now carried out by both dividers and compasses. Three uses are present here: measuring or dividing the distance between two points;

opening and subsequently closing the compasses in the course of taking a measurement, and drawing a circle.

The precision and detail of this conceit provokes a number of questions. Does the detail enhance or detract from the poem as a whole? Is the precision an embodiment of the firm control of emotion for which the poet so beguilingly pleads? Is the conceit too cold and austere? Is the attention necessary to appreciate the conceit out of proportion to the space it occupies in the poem?

36 **end, where I begun**   is the image of a circle being completed less satisfactory as a symbol of homecoming than the closing of compasses (29–36)?

A Valediction: of Weeping

Parting before a journey is the subject of several Donne poems. As in the case of *Song: Sweetest love* and *A Valediction: forbidding Mourning*, this poem makes the standard poetic connections between sea and tears and wind and sighs. Yet whereas these connections were passing references in the *Song* and the mourning *Valediction*, here the conceit of tears is the chief matter of the poem. And as the chief matter, other conceits (perhaps all of them) are derived from it. Donne draws our attention to this by saying of tears that they are *emblems of more* (7). Understandably, J.B. Leishman called the poem 'fiendishly ingenious'. Is it any more than that?

Title Weeping and tears were popular subjects in sixteenth- and seventeenth-century poetry.

   2 **My tears**   readers need to work out who is weeping and when.

3–4 Look through these lines to see how the image of tears produces a conceit on coins.

   6 **pregnant**   what is it about this image that makes it appropriate at this point in the poem? The same question can be asked of line 2 in *The Ecstasy*.

   7 **emblems of more**   see the introductory note.

8 **that thou** that person.
9 **nothing** consider the emotional impact of this word in the
poem as a whole. If they are nothing, then there are no tears
and if no tears, no poem.
divers shore in a different country.
10–13 Edward Wright (1558–1615) worked out the mathematics that
enabled mapmakers to project flat shapes onto a sphere. The
workman (11) had to use several sheets of paper (*copies*).
13 **nothing** Because a *globe* (16) is round it is like a nought and is
therefore *nothing*.
16 **impression** see note on lines 3–4.
17–18 A conceit based on the Biblical Flood (Genesis: 6–9) is present
here.
18 **my heaven** the poet's beloved.
20 **draw not up seas** the moon controls the tides.
21 **in thine arms** what is the effect of knowing that he is lying in
her arms?
26 **one another's breath** the mutual breathing (and, of course,
kissing) of couples was used as an image of the departure of
breath in dying, hence *hastes each other's breath*, (27). See *The
Expiration*.

Woman's Constancy

This poem is a game played between poet, mistress and reader,
with neither mistress nor reader being quite sure what the poet is
going to say next. We are not sure, because the poem seems to
combine an edgy uncertainty with an impulse to mock and
ridicule. Reading the poem aloud might bring out the difficulties
of judging its tone. How, for instance, should *whole* (1), *now* (4)
and *just* (5) be delivered?

Title How applicable is the title?
2 **when thou leav'st** is the tone one of sad resignation in the
face of female infidelity, or can you detect the deliberate
adoption of the pose of a hurt man?
say it is important to ask whether the real subject matter is

not what people do but the words they use.

3 **antedate**   to assign an earlier date to an event or agreement.

4–13 Do the four sentences beginning with *Or* suggest the woman's remarkable capacity for argument, the poet's bitter realization of just how fickle the woman is, or are they arguments the man puts into the woman's mouth in order to prepare for the reversal with which the poem ends?

10 **sleep, death's image**   it was a poetic convention that sleep was akin to death.

14 **lunatic**   she might be a lunatic because she foolishly wants to abandon her lover or because, like the moon, she is changeable.
'scapes   tricks or wiles often prompted by sexual motives.

15 **Dispute, and conquer**   is the aggressively masculine edge of these words blunted by the nonchalant and even indifferent tone of the couplet in which they appear?

16 **abstain**   how surprising is his refusal to tackle the arguments of his fickle mistress? Might we reflect that the poem has shown that the words of lovers are unreliable?

Elegy 4: The Perfume

This poem is akin to a domestic comedy such as was written by Donne's contemporary, Ben Jonson. An adventurous young man courts a girl, who, in the traditions of comedy, is locked up by her jealous family, but although he evades the *hydroptic father* (6), the *immortal mother* (13) and *The grim eight-foot-high iron-bound serving-man* (31) (all of them like characters from a comedy) he is, with delightful comic irony, given away by his own *loud perfume* (41). Donne creates a distinctive persona, whose enterprising but luckless escapades are related in appropriately rough couplets. Perhaps there are moments, so common in Donne, when an interest in arguments and ideas dilutes the psychological consistency of the persona.

2 **escapes** adventurous escapades of an amorous nature.
3–6 The tone of hurt outrage is evident in the spiteful remark about her *hydroptic* (6) (suffering from dropsy) father, yet perhaps there is also pride and even enjoyment in being singled out as the object of her father's anger? Does the emphatic swagger of *So am I* (5) indicate his pleasure at being the centre of interest?
3 **at bar** in a criminal court the accused stands at the bar.
7–8 The *cockatrice* or basilisk is a kind of lizard which was believed to kill by its looks. Is her father so fierce that he can even kill a cockatrice, or are his eyes so old and his vision so bleary (*glazed* could have that meaning) that spying on the lovers is as likely to be as successful as trying to outstare a *cockatrice*?
11 **Hope of his goods** Who is after what? The young man might be accusing the father of only being interested in his daughter's price on the marriage market. He might also be quoting the father's view that the lover is only interested in her riches. And what does the reader make of the lover? Is he a trustworthy man motivated by love or a daring opportunist out for sexual pleasure?
14 **buried in her bed** a play on the traditional association between the grave and the bed.
18 **rings... armlets** love tokens.

20 **swoll'n** pregnant. See note on *The Flea* (8).

21–2 The mother is closely watching her daughter for signs of pregnancy such as a pale complexion or a sudden liking for a particular food.

23 **politicly** scheming with the ulterior motive of securing a confession of guilt from her daughter.

25–26 This couplet brings the poem very close to comedy. Many comic plots depend upon the ability of the young to *gull* (deceive, mislead or cheat) unwary adults. Audiences are usually invited to find the adventurous young attractive. Is that the case here?

29 **ingled** dandled or fondled by their father.

34 **Rhodian Colossus** the Colossus of Rhodes (one of the seven wonders of the ancient world) was an enormous statue that was said to stand across the entrance to Rhodes harbour.

41 **loud** look through the poem for words that are a contrast to *loud*.

47–9 The *isle* of Britain, where the native beasts are cattle and dogs rather than the exotic *unicorn*.

52 **oppressed** this probably refers to pressing prisoners with heavy weights to make them talk.

53–70 Perhaps the simulated fury of this long denunciation of perfume contributes to the comedy of the poem. Do we also feel Donne's intellectual pleasure in formulating such a dramatic and intricate expression of the persona's plight?

57 **Base excrement** it was a popular joke that perfume was merely the excretion of flowers and animals.

59 **silly amorous** a foolish lover.

64 **substantial** real, solid things overlooked by those in a Prince's court, who are distracted by empty fashion.

67–8 **simply... joined** things made up of loathsome separate (*simply*) entities are no better when made into a compound (*joined*).

70 **rare** good things are universal not unusual (*rare*) as is perfume.

71–2 Perhaps the closing couplet has the quality of an afterthought. It does, however, return to the plight of the lover being frustrated by the father and provides, with a dash of grim wit, a new use for the perfume.

72 **corse** corpse.

Elegy 5: His Picture

This elegy observes some of the conventions of contemporary poetry: separated lovers are spoken of as *dead* (3), and those united by a deep love speak of themselves as superior to *rival fools* (11). What makes it characteristically Donne's is its blend of vivid physical detail and quasi-theological argument. As so often in Donne, the balance or tension of these elements gives the poem life.

1 **picture** miniature portraits, often no wider than 4 to 5 centimetres, were commonly given as parting gifts.

3 **dead** can this be read both metaphorically and literally?

4 **shadows** a picture could be spoken of as a shadow. A ghost or shade could also be called a shadow.

5–10 Perhaps because writing as visual as this is rare in Donne, readers might find these lines more interesting, and even more convincing, than the passage that follows about how love can look beyond appearances to the inner self.

10 **powder** gunpowder.

13 **This** the portrait.

and thou shalt say how convincing is this? Does he have complete confidence in the maturity of her love and so can predict how she will react, or is he aware of how repulsive he might be and so is leading her to respond in a way which is favourable to him?

18 **milk** in the Bible and in much religious literature it is common to draw a distinction between the spiritually young who, like babies, need milk and the mature who can feed on the real meat of religion. For instance: *I gave you milk to drink, and not meat*, I Corinthians 3:1.

Elegy 16: On his Mistress

The beloved's wish to accompany the poet makes her more like the heroine of a romantic, even a Shakespearean, comedy, who disguises herself in order to be with the man she loves. Donne, however, departs from the plot conventions of romantic comedy by having the lover persuade his beloved not to adopt the role of the disguised heroine. It is a highly wrought piece with many repetitions and carefully paced climaxes, yet, as with many Donne poems, such an elaborate patterning in the language exists alongside what seems to be genuine feeling; note, for instance, the touching simplicity of the close.

1 **fatal** this word could point to the depth of their love by implying that even at their first meeting (*interview*) they were destined for each other, and it might also anticipate the fears of his death, which are the subject of lines 50–4.

3 **remorse** the tenderness and pity she feels for him.

4 **my words' masculine persuasive force** so much of Donne is in these words: a self-centred celebration of his prowess in loving, a knowledge of how his beloved will respond to his persuasion, and, given *words'*, an awareness of the power of his poetry.

7 **calmly** should the poet be believed when he says he begs *calmly*?

8 **want and divorcement** her absence from him due to separation.

11 **overswear** swears oaths of constant love again and again.

14 His insistence that she should not disguise herself and follow him is consistent with his firm statement in line 12 that she *shalt not love by ways so dangerous*. It is difficult to know how a reader should respond. Do we admire his concern that she be treated with the dignity of a *true mistress*, or might we regret that he is denying her the brave and enterprising role of the *feigned page*?

16 **only** this means either that she is the only one who could rouse in him the *thirst* (17) to return or that that is the only role she can play.

19 **move** remove.

21–3 Donne appears to be recasting a Greek myth here: instead of *Boreas* (21) – the north wind – carrying away a girl called *Orithea* (23), he makes *Orithea* a tree or plant, which is *in pieces shivered* (22) by *Boreas*.

24 **proved** undergone or suffered.

25 **unurged** without compulsion or necessity.

27 **Dissemble nothing** the immediate meaning is: do not disguise yourself. Can, however, the idea of other sorts of deception be excluded?

28 **strange** to be either a stranger or to be someone whose identity is concealed. *Strange* has appeared in line 1.

30 This line can be usefully compared with line 4. We might also ask whether such polarized understandings of men and women are found in other poems?

31 **apes** fools. The point of comparison is based on the proverb that apes are still apes even if they are richly dressed.

33 **chameleons** in the same way that chameleons change their colour, so the French change their moods.

34 **Spitals of diseases** a spital is a hospital, which treated venereal diseases.

35 **Love's fuellers** those who stoke up their own passions.

36 **players** the poet criticizes the French for being players, but he and his beloved might also be said to play.

37 **know** does the poet successfully play upon the two meanings of *know* – recognize and have sexual intercourse with?

38 **indifferent** oblivious as to whether his lust is satisfied by either man or woman.

41 **Lot** in Genesis 19: 4–11 the men of Sodom are so aroused by two angels who visit Lot that they demand that Lot hand them over so they can satisfy their lust.

42 **spongy hydroptic** see *A Nocturnal upon S. Lucy's Day, being the shortest day* (6).

43–6 A *gallery* (44) is a long room, often found in palaces or mansions, which adjoined the main room of the house. If the King were present, those wishing to see him would have to wait in the gallery. The image might be an allegory in which the soul waits to be called into God's presence or it could show life in England to be attractive in comparison with the moral squalor of the Continent.

47 Compare this with the last stanza of *Song: Sweetest love*.

51–4 How should this outburst be understood? Does it show he knows her so well he understands her fears, or does a phrase such as the *white Alps alone* (53) indicate he finds the prospect of travel exciting?

55 **Augur**   forecast or predict.
   except   unless.
   dread Jove   God, but perhaps with a hint of the wilfulness
   and unpredictability associated with Greek and Roman gods.

Elegy 19: To his Mistress Going to Bed

This is a poem about anticipation. As the title states, it is about
Going to Bed rather than what happens in it. Perhaps as a result
of this, the poet's mind interestingly explores a wide range of
ideas and associations. There is religious speculation, imagery
about colonial adventures and an intellectually complex
discourse on nakedness. Is his mind more active than his hands?
Readers are often surprised at how frank and detailed the poem
is (think about all those layers of clothes). Yet is it a sensuously
arousing piece? And though the scene itself is detailed, there is
much that we do not know. Is the woman his wife (perhaps this
is her wedding-night), his mistress or a prostitute? Is it possible
to imagine the events that led up to this encounter?

1 **Come**   poems which are invitations to love often start with or
   emphasize this word.
   my   is the character of the poem indicated by the prominent
   use of the personal pronouns? Think about the rhyming of
   my... defy... I... I... lie. They might be read as assertively male
   or as sighs, as in sounds of the fourth stanza of *Song: Sweetest
   love.*
2 **labour... in labour lie**   the first *labour* means sexual activity,
   the second agonized anticipation.
3 **The foe**   military language was often used in love poems. Does
   it make the poem playful or emotionally antagonistic? The
   sexual joking in the poem might point to the former possibility,
   while the grammar (the poet gives orders) may lend support to
   the latter view.
4 **standing**   here, as in lines 11–12 and 23–4, the poet calls
   attention to his erect penis. Does this frankness create an erotic

atmosphere or, given the unease about sustaining an erection (*tired*), is there the glimpse of an anxious lover, who suffers from self-doubt?

5 **heaven's zone**   the Milky Way.

6 **a far fairer world**   the woman's body is seen as a *world*. Might this signify how wonderful she is, or that his desire is to discover, exploit and conquer?

7 **spangled breastplate**   ladies often wore jewelled stomachers, which covered their breasts.

9 **harmonious chime**   either the jingling of the jewels or her chiming watch.

11 **busk**   corset.

15 **wiry coronet**   a decorative band of metal worn round the brow.

16 **hairy diadem**   since diadems were associated with royalty, the implication may be that her natural beauty, in this case her hair, exceeds the beauty of her *coronet* (15) How important is this idea in the poem as a whole?

17–18 removing shoes is a religious act, performed when entering a holy place. Such language raises the issue of whether we are invited to view sexual union as a holy act. Consider Wilbur Sanders' view that this poem stands nearer to 'religion than all the conscious spirituality of *The Ecstasy*'.

21 **Mahomet's paradise**   Donne follows the uninformed popular view that Moslems imagined that in paradise there was endless sexual pleasure.

22 **Ill spirits walk in white**   Donne's contemporaries believed that it was often exceedingly difficult to tell a good from an evil spirit, because evil spirits were often disguised as good ones, that is, they appeared in angelic white. See note on 24.

23 **sprite**   spirit.

24 **hairs... flesh**   the idea here is that an erection enables the lover to distinguish between good and evil spirits. Some readers might find this a disappointing crudity; others might enjoy the wit of such a simple solution.

25 **License**   allow, but possibly also the idea of taking out a licence for mining or other kinds of economic exploitation.

27 Different parts of America were described as new-found lands.

29 **empery**   empire.

30 **discovering**   uncovering.

31 **bonds**   her loving arms that will hold him fast, a legal agreement or, even, the *bonds* of indissoluble marriage.

32 **seal**   this usually refers to the sexual organs, as in *The Relic* (29–30). The word also refers to the sealing of a legal document.

34–5 Again, Donne uses religious language. The lover might feel a kind of religious wonder in the presence of his naked mistress, and he might also enjoy the oddity of comparing naked bodies to souls without bodies.

35–8 Donne alters the story of Hippomenes, who distracted Atalanta in a race by throwing golden balls in her way, by making Atalanta the one who distracted men by throwing down jewels. The lines leave it unclear as to who exactly is the fool.

40 **laymen**   the idea here is that ordinary men (*laymen*) need pictures or fine bindings, whereas real scholars do not.

41–3 True lovers are like a small band of religious believers. Lovers only see their beloved's nakedness *revealed* if she grants them the privilege, and believers are only counted righteous (*imputed*) by God and are thus able to understand the revelations of the Bible (*mystic books*). (See *Holy Sonnet 6*, 13.) One of the critical issues of this poem is how we should take this conceit.

44 **midwife**   is the word suitable? For a similar problem, see *The Flea* (8).

46 **penance... innocence**   the implication is that although she wears white she might be neither penitent (those guilty of sexual crimes did public penance in white garments) nor innocent of sexual experience. Is the lover pleased she is not innocent?

48 **covering**   the difficulty here is that this word was customarily used of the copulation of horses and not people.

Holy Sonnet 6

In the octave of this sonnet (1–8) the poet creates in detail the intense musings of a man anticipating his own death, and in the cooler and more theological sestet (9–14) he attempts to calm the fears aroused by the opening through the consoling hope of imputed righteousness. Should we praise the octave's vivid imagery and high emotional temperature, or be more impressed by the intellectual clarity of the sestet, which is more humble and self-aware than the octave's heated, theatrical rhetoric?

1–4 Might rapidly moving from one image to another show a fascination with death, a fear so intense that he desperately seeks to control it through a series of vivid and familiar images or a dramatization of his plight to bring out how serious it is?

5 **gluttonous death** a reader might recoil in horror from the image of death as a predatory but otherwise hardly focused creature, who will *instantly unjoint* (5) body and soul. But can we exclude the grotesque humour of death as a glutton (*gluttonous*) or a butcher (*unjoint*)?

7 **that face** what face? There are several answers: God, death, the devil. Does this range of possible meanings enrich the poem?

13 **Impute me righteous** this essentially Anglican (rather than Roman Catholic) doctrine argues that as Adam's sin, due to the fall, is attributed, or imputed, to all, salvation is only possible if people are correspondingly imputed righteous by the merits of Christ's suffering and death upon the cross. The sermon in the *Second Book of Homilies* (1563) on justification contains this remark: 'we cannot be accounted righteous, but by Christ's merits imputed to us'.

14 **For thus I leave** the significance of the theatrical close (it is like an actor's dramatic exit) depends upon whether the poet confidently departs, knowing he has been imputed righteous. If, however, it is an histrionic (the gesture of an actor) movement, the reader might see just how in need of mercy this self-regarding poet is.

The words *the world, the flesh, and devil* are a reference to the Baptism Service in *The Book of Common Prayer*. They might indicate that, as at baptism, the sins have been renounced or that he draws attention to his still fallen state to strengthen his plea for mercy.

Holy Sonnet 7

There are striking contrasts between the octave and the sestet. The opening is colourful, highly peopled and even theatrical, whereas what follows is visually spare and highly individualistic. The tone changes from bold gestures (it is as if he, rather than God, announces the Last Judgement) to low-key requests that God teaches him how to repent.

1 **round earth's imagined corners** The image combines the roundness of the earth with words from the last book of the Bible: 'four angels standing at the four corners of the earth' (Revelation 7.1). Perhaps the deliberate strangeness of the language is appropriate to an event so unparalleled that words have to be stretched and extended beyond their ordinary meanings in order to imagine it.

4 **to your scattered bodies go** at the last Judgement souls will be reunited with their bodies.

5 **flood... fire** *flood* refers to Genesis 6–8 (the first book in the Bible) and *fire* to Revelation 8. What does this time span from beginning to end contribute to the poem?

6 **agues** diseases.

9 **But let them sleep, Lord** These words create a problem typical of Donne's religious verse. Is this impudent blasphemy, or the uncertain humour of a man aware of the gulf between him and Christ?

10 **abound** in Romans 5:20 St Paul writes: 'where sin abounded, there grace abounded much more'.

12 **there; here** does this simple placing together enhance or detract from the gravity of the sonnet?

13–14 The tone here is difficult. The almost colloquial *for that's as good* might indicate either confidence or nervous bluster. Likewise, Christian doctrine asserts that Christ has sealed everybody's pardon with the blood of the cross, yet the effect of *As if* might make the final line sound more tentative.

Holy Sonnet 10

This sonnet may be read as a poetic duel with death, in which word-play corresponds to skilful swordsmanship, and variations in pace and emotional intensity to the thrusts and parries of the poet's attack and defence. (The last sermon Donne preached to the court of King Charles I was called *Death's Duel*.) It is difficult to characterize the overall tone: is he serious in the face of a mighty foe, cosily intimate and even casually witty at death's expense or denigrating almost to the extent of being sneering? Another problem is that the argument is clearly false, being based on analogies such as the conventional one between sleep and death. It might be said in defence that the poem tackles not death but the language we use of it – *though some have called thee/Mighty and dreadful* (1–2). Perhaps we value the poem not for its argument but the convincing creation of an anxious mind bracing itself against death with a variety of images.

1 **proud**   the word has the sense of being outstanding and awe-inspiring as well as boastfully self-confident. Both senses are also present in *swell'st* (12).

4 **nor yet canst thou kill me**   the quickened pace of these heavily stressed monosyllables might suggest a lively confidence that the poet has the measure of his opponent, or they could be a defensive thrust at a strong adversary, whom he fears.

8 **delivery**   the soul is delivered in the sense that at death it is born into eternity and so delivered from the prison of life.

13 **wake eternally**   wake to the presence of God. Is there a quiet confidence in the restraint of such language that is more appealing and religiously profound than the direct appeals of, for instance, *Holy Sonnet 14*?

14 **Death thou shalt die**   is this an effective end to the poem? Is it inconsistent to write off the fear of death only to serve it up as a threat to Death itself? A defence might be that to die is to pass to a realm, where Death is no more.

Holy Sonnet 13

The tension, as in so many Donne poems, is between divine and earthly love. In the intensely realized presentation of the crucified Christ, Donne may be, as elsewhere, dependent upon traditions of religious meditation in which those who prayed pictured in their imaginations scenes from the Bible. By contrast, the sestet is relaxed and even casual; we might imagine the poet confidently shaking his head in *No, no; but as in my idolatry* (9). As with most of the sonnets, it is important to see how the close settles the intellectual and emotional energies.

2 **Mark** the word had contemplative and meditative connotations.

4 **countenance** in the Bible this word is frequently used of God's face: 'The Lord lift up his countenance upon thee' (Numbers 6:26). Think about how Donne writes about the face of God and the face of his beloveds.

5 **amazing** frightening or even horrifying.

6 **pierced head** see St Mark 15:17: 'and platted a crown of thorns and put it about his head'.

8 **forgiveness** see St Luke's account of the crucifixion: 'Jesus said, Father, forgive them; for they know not what they do' (23:34).

10 **profane mistresses** he worshipped women as if they were divine. Does the argument of the sonnet depend upon a contrast or a comparison between Christ and his *profane mistresses*?

11–12 the idea is that only ugly women have no pity on ardent lovers.

14 **This beauteous form** Christ is both beautiful and full of pity. How far is the beauty of Christ from the beauty of his *profane mistresses* (10)?

Holy Sonnet 14

Nowhere else in Donne's religious poetry is the drama and the contradictory violence of paradox so evident as in this sonnet. There is something thrilling, even exhilarating, about the lightness and speed of the poet's thought and the way the paradoxes mount to the breathtaking and outrageous climax of the closing couplet. Is Donne attempting to renew a jaded religious language? Is the poem in danger of delighting in contradictions?

1 **my... you**   as in many of the love poems, the frequency and impact of the first and second person pronouns is important.

2,4 The lines contrast *Break, blow, burn* (4) with *knock, breathe, shine* (2). Some of the words have strong biblical associations. Christ in Revelation 3:20 says: 'Behold I stand at the door and knock', and in St Matthew 6:19 it is 'thieves who break through and steal'.

5 **usurped town**   a town in which power has illegally (and probably violently) passed from a legitimate ruler to an invader.
 another   it is not clear who or what *another* is; it could be the devil, death, sin, doubt, despair or a human lover.

7 **viceroy**   one who wields power on behalf of a supreme (and usually absent) ruler.

9 **fain**   willingly or gladly.

11 **Divorce**   this word is central to an implied story, which acts as a parallel to the poet's religious state: a woman has desperately fallen in love (9) but is betrothed, married or has been stolen by another so cannot be *free* (13) or *chaste* (14) (the word was applied to married couples) until her true love divorces her from the one to whom she is bound. But the idea is hardly Christian. The Anglican marriage service insists: 'Those whom God hath joined together let no man put asunder.' Can the word *divorce* ever be appropriately used of God's relationships with his people?

Holy Sonnet 17

This is a poem of strong feelings, which the poet hardly seems to fully understand. Perhaps its expression of uncertainty is what makes it successful. Is it, for example, about human or divine love? It also seems unfinished. Lines 9–14 set out God's attitude to the poet (9–14), but no response is given.

Donne's biography may be relevant here. His wife, Ann Donne, died on 15 August 1617, seven days after giving birth to their twelfth child. She was 33. The poem might not have been written immediately afterwards; Helen Gardner thinks that it might date from 1619.

1–4   The logical use of *Since* and the conventional characterization of death as paying a *debt/To nature* might suggest that the poet accepts his loss with little or no anguish. But the heavy stresses at the end of the first line and the way the rhythm singles out the painful word *early* (3) could indicate a deeply-felt grief.

3   **ravished**   carried away into heaven.

4   **Wholly**   is there a pun on holy?

5   **whet**   sharpen and make ready.

6   **seek thee God**   try to hear how the cadence leads to the word *God*. Are there stronger climaxes in the poem?

8   **A holy thirsty dropsy melts me**   the language is poised between divine and earthly love. The words *thirsty* and *dropsy* apply to both, though *melts* (emotionally affects) is more appropriate to love poetry.

9–10   God is cast in the role of a father who supplies the dowry of Christ's love (*offering all thine*) to bring about the heavenly marriage of the poet and his dead beloved.

13   **tender jealousy**   God is presented in the Bible as jealous; that is, as holding on to what is rightly his. What does *tender* add to this idea? See *A Hymn to Christ, at the Author's last going into Germany*, 20.

    doubt   fear and suspect.

Holy Sonnet 19

Instead of images of the Last Judgement, the figure of Death or the crucified Christ, the poet, through rapid changes in tone, pace and cadence, expresses puzzlement at his own spiritual state. Does this narrower range make it less impressive than other *Holy Sonnets*? The phrase *contraries meet in one* is a good description of the tensions of the poem as well as of the spiritual state of the poet.

1 **vex**   the word had a much stronger meaning in the seventeenth century than it has today, being closer to shaken with anguish.

2–3 **Inconstancy/constant**   what is the effect of this verbal playing upon the poet's distress?

4 **vows**   the relationship between religious poetry and love poetry which emerges in some of the *Holy Sonnets* is present in this and other words in the poem.

5 **humorous**   changeable.
   Contrition   being sorry for one's sins.

7 **riddlingly distempered**   his contrition wildly swings from one extreme to another as if he were unbalanced by disease.

9 **I durst**   unlike some of the other *Holy Sonnets*, there is not a sharp break between the octave and the sestet. Does this make it an impressively concentrated poem, or do you miss the drama of a change from one mood to another?

11 **rod**   God's justice and punishment are frequently spoken of as a rod.

13 **fantastic**   uncertain, extreme, unpredictable.
   ague   a disease or fever.

13–14 Does the paradox of his *best days* (a phrase often used when talking about health) being those when he *shake(s) with fear* successfully sum up the *contraries* (1) of the poem?

Good Friday, 1613. Riding Westward

This poem, which opens with intellectual speculation and closes with an ardent plea that God will redeem him, typically blends a poetic realization that his westward journey accurately mirrors the state of his relationship to God with an anguished realization of how serious that relationship is. In keeping with the poetic or fabricated nature of the poem, what is seen is the product not of the physical eye but of the imagination. In line 33 he says that the Cross of Christ is far *from mine eye*, and in line 35 there is a telling picture of the guilty poet with his back to Christ yet his memory fixed on him.

1–10   Donne works with the astronomical theory that each planet consisted of a sphere controlled by an intelligence or spirit. Planets could come under the influence of another more powerful agent and so be governed by it rather than following their natural course – (*natural form*) (6). The natural direction was from west to east, but so powerful was the Primum Mobile (in Donne's analogy the *first mover*, line 8) that they actually travelled in the reverse direction.

8   **whirled**   there might be a pun here.

11   **sun**   another pun?
    rising   *rising* could mean the incarnation of Christ, the physical lifting up of the cross or the resurrection.

13   **But that**   except that.

17   This is a common Biblical idea: 'Thou canst not see my face: for there shall no man see me and live' (Exodus 33:20).

19–20   The New Testament says that the crucifixion of Jesus was accompanied by darkness – 'darkness over all the land' (St Matthew 27:45), and that at his death there was an earthquake – 'and the earth did shake, and the stones were cloven' (St Matthew 27:51). The word *lieutenant* is Donne's own metaphor for nature as God's second in command; *footstool* is a Biblical metaphor for the earth being under God's authority – 'the earth is my footstool' (Isaiah 66:1).

24   **Zenith... antipodes**   wherever one is on earth (*antipodes* means its furthest points), God is an absolute distance from us.

25–6   Some believed that souls had their seat or basis in blood, though theologians questioned whether this could apply to Christ (*if not of his*). They agreed, however, that since salvation came through the cross, all souls rested in Christ's blood.

29–32   There is an ancient practice of contemplating the figure of Mary, the Mother of Jesus, at the foot of the cross. Mary was God's partner, because she agreed to bear the Christ child, and thus she provided *Half of that sacrifice* by which the world was redeemed (*ransomed*).

36   **tree**   the cross.

37   **but**   only.

38   **Corrections**   punishments aimed at reforming him.
    leave   stop.

39–40   Compare the violence of these pleas (demands?) with the language of *Holy Sonnet 14* (1–4). How strong in both is the idea that the poet would rather be the object of God's anger than be ignored?

41 **Restore thine image** salvation was thought of as a return to mankind's original estate, when the image of God was clearly present in people.

A Hymn to Christ, at the Author's last going into Germany

In this grave poem, the poet examines his spiritual state. We hear him meditating on its seriousness in the strong monosyllabic thrust of many of the words. Through a consideration of such weighty issues as death, providence, and the nature of love, he moves towards a climactic decision. Because there are many ideas and the pace is fast, readers will need to take their time with it.

Title On 12 May 1619 Donne sailed as chaplain with the Earl of Doncaster's diplomatic mission to the German Princes. Shortly before he left he preached a farewell sermon at Lincoln's Inn in which he spoke of Christ and the sea: *Sea of his blood.*

2 **my emblem of thy ark** an emblem was a visual representation of a quality or idea in a system of thought; it was usually used as a teaching device and was often accompanied by a woodcut and a short poem giving a moral comment. Here the poet makes a traditional association between a ship and Noah's ark, which survived the Flood. The ark is emblematic of Divine providence and the Church.

4 **blood** the word *blood* stands for the redemption of mankind by the cross of Christ.

8 **never** is the emphatic stress on *never* one of unswerving conviction, or is there an element of bravado in it, possibly arising from doubt or fear?

9 **sacrifice** the word *sacrifice* includes the idea that he renounces his earthly and temporal loves and that he gives them, or offers them, to God.
Island England.

12 **thy sea**   see note on line 4.

14 **winter**   the word suggests age, the loss of earthly pleasure and the absence of his own inner, or spiritual, resources. Thus, in a line that effectively says he is nothing, Donne characteristically plays on the multiple meanings of a word.

17 **control**   in a soul which is whole and integrated (*harmonious*) there is no need for Christ or the Church to check or restrain (*control*) its love.

18 **amorousness**   this word might suggest earthly and even erotic love rather than the love the soul has for God. As with many of Donne's poems, we might ask whether there is a struggle over the renunciation of earthly ties or a similarity between sexual love and the love of God.

20 **jealous**   the idea that God possessively loves and guards all that belongs to him frequently occurs in the Bible: 'for 1 am the Lord, thy God, a jealous God' (Exodus 20:5). Here Christ is the jealous lover.

21–2 See *Holy Sonnet 17* (9–10).

22 **who ever gives, takes liberty**   this can mean both that giving one's love is not always justified (that is, one takes a liberty in doing so) and that whoever gives someone love takes away that person's freedom.

25 **divorce**   see note on *Holy Sonnet 14* (11).

26 **fainter beams**   the beams of the sun are often symbols of God's or Christ's (there is a pun on son) love for the world.

28 **hopes**   worldly prospects such as a place in the life of the court.

29 Consider the place in this and other religious poems of how negation – lack of light, lack of love, lack of success – is the way to God. To what extent in Donne is it the absence of things (even the absence of religious experience) that brings the poet to God?

30 **I go out of sight**   this could mean 'I travel far away' and 'I die'.

32 Does the dark and long falling cadence close the poem heavily and gloomily, or is there a distinctive triumph in that the poet has freely chosen *night* rather than worldly pleasures (28), knowing it will bring him to God?

Hymn to God my God, in my Sickness

Perhaps the most remarkable aspect of this poem is its serene tone. There is no apparent anguish, and, unlike some of the Holy Sonnets, the many paradoxes and polarities (for instance: *do / think* (5), *west / east* (13), *death / resurrection* (15)) are not born out of spiritual turmoil, and, what is more, they are neatly resolved. Such neatness makes the poem intellectually elegant; to use a metaphor from the poem itself, everything is mapped out with a satisfying clarity. Even the potential violence of the last line could be allayed by seeing that the idea is not a sudden dramatic outburst but a text carefully chosen by the preacher in which *throws down* is balanced by the religiously important word *raise*. Perhaps the poem captures the experience that many sick or dying people have of being happily released from the body's pain and free to view themselves in a detached and spiritually calm way.

Title   Isaac Walton claimed that the poem was written during
       Donne's final illness in 1631, but it may have been composed
       during or shortly after a serious illness he suffered in 1623.

1   **holy room**   heaven.

4   **I tune the instrument**   a musician, being only an employee,
    would tune his instrument before entering the banqueting hall
    of a mansion. The image might mean prepare oneself with
    prayers before death or practise the art of poetry so that the
    harmony of verse may anticipate the harmony of the *choir of*
    saints (2).

5   **before**   this word draws attention to how the opening stanza is
    separated from the others: how should the relation between it
    and the rest of the poem be understood? Does the musical
    imagery successfully prepare us for the emotionally composed
    and serene tone of the poem, or is the jump from a domestic
    setting to the furthest parts of the world so extreme as to cut
    this stanza off damagingly from the rest?

6   **love**   the doctors' loving concern for him.

7   **Cosmographers... map**   because, according to a common
    contemporary idea, a person was a little world, it is poetically

appropriate to see his physicians as geographers (*cosmographers*) examining a *map* of the world.

9 **my south-west discovery** a *discovery* was a passage or route into distant parts of the world. Here the geographical image functions figuratively: south is the region of heat and west is where the sun sets; that is to say, he expects to die as the result of a fever.

10 **Per fretum febris** this means both 'through the raging fever' and 'through the strait of fever'.

straits this can mean a narrow passage of sea water, the trials and difficulties of life and the hard way to salvation.

11 **I joy** is the poet fully aware of his plight and yet able to rejoice at the prospect of death, or is he only confident because he has avoided the reality of death by, so to speak, disguising it in elegant and intellectually clever imagery?

13–14 Donne makes this point in one of his sermons: 'but to paste that flat Map upon a round body, and then West and East are all one'. In theological terms *west* is death and *east* symbolizes the resurrection. See note on lines 10–13 in *A Valediction: of Weeping*.

16–17 There was a centuries-old debate about the geographical location of Eden, the earthly paradise. As Eden was a mirror of Heaven, the images and emblems of these lines are all associated with Paradise. *Pacific* means peaceful; *Jerusalem*, as well as being an image of the heavenly city, also means vision of peace, and *eastern riches* is reminiscent of the imagery in the Gospels for the Kingdom of Heaven – treasure and great pearls.

18 The *Anyan* straits were supposed to separate North America from Asia. The straits of *Magellan* are at the foot of South America, and the Mediterranean Sea is entered through the straits of *Gibraltar*.

20 It was traditionally believed that after the Biblical flood the world was divided between the sons of Noah: Japheth (*Japhet*) was given Europe, Ham (*Cham*) Africa and *Shem* Asia.

21–2 The conceit of the map leads to the much debated issue of where Paradise was located (16–17). Donne explores the widespread belief that since Eden was in the region of Mesopotamia, it was in the same location (*stood in one place*) as

Jerusalem, where Christ was crucified. There are also legends about how the wood for Christ's cross came from a tree that grew out of the bones of Adam. St Paul compares Adam to Christ; for instance: 'For as in Adam all die, even so in Christ shall all be made alive' (I Corinthians 15:22). Christ is also the 'last Adam' (I Corinthians 15:45).

24 **sweat** because Adam brought death into the world through the fall, the poet's feverish sweat is that of the first Adam.

25 **blood** see note on *A Hymn to Christ, at the Author's last going into Germany* (4).

26 **purple** the conceit is that Christ's blood is like a robe of royal purple.

27 **thorns... other crown** thorns could mean the crown of thorns which Christ wore when he brought about salvation on the cross, and the poet might figuratively be referring to his own sufferings as being like a crown of thorns. The *other crown* is the heavenly crown worn by those in heaven.

29 **to mine own** to myself.

30 Strictly speaking this is not a Biblical text. Nevertheless, it reflects Biblical thinking in its paradox that those who are raised are those that have been thrown down.

A Hymn to God the Father

Walton records that this poem was written during Donne's illness of 1623. Its tone, imagery, argument and manner may, therefore, be usefully compared to *Hymn to God my God, in my Sickness*, which may have been written at the same time. The movement and tone are memorable: its pace is measured, and in the gravity and honesty of its brooding self-questioning there is a dark yet dignified progress towards the final plea and the undemonstrative assurance of the close. The big problem of the poem is whether the tone is consistently maintained. Is this a poem in which the mind of the poet is concentrated with moving seriousness upon his relationship with God, or is he, at points, preoccupied with his own skill as a poet, who exploits the possibilities of language?

Title Why is the poem addressed to God the Father? In the closing
stanza there is a pun on Christ as the Son of God and the sun:
should the poem be read as being about the salvation brought
by the Son of God, or should it be interpreted as the humble
request of a man who wants God the Father to accept him as a
son? Can it be both?

1–12 There are four questions in the first two stanzas; if you try
reading them aloud you may notice that, unusually, the final
cadence falls rather than rises. What is the effect of this? Does
it suggest that the poet is assured of salvation so the question is
not a real one or, conversely, that he is so absorbed in
meditating upon his unworthiness that he dare not question
God in an ordinary way?

1 **begun** according to Christian doctrine, humanity is marked
by the fall of Adam (Genesis 3) and thus bears his guilt. This is
called original sin. It was sometimes thought of as being
transmitted from one generation to another through
procreation. Hence when he *begun* he was a sinner.

5 **done** should a man who is so aware of his need for God's
mercy allow himself the poetic indulgence of a pun on his own
name? Is the introduction of the pun a flaw, because it detracts
from the weighty seriousness of the poem's tone? It might be
argued that it is a daring and successful way of showing how
delightful it would be to be possessed and owned by God.

6 **more** some critics detect a pun on Donne's wife's name –
Ann More.

7 **that sin** the sin could be any wrong deed that led others
astray, and, more specifically, the writing of sexually explicit
poetry.

10 **wallowed** this could be a comic moment of self-mockery, in
which he pictures himself grotesquely indulging in sin.
Another possibility is that as there is a traditional association
between wallowing and pigs, the poet is imagining himself in
the role of the prodigal son (St Luke 15:11–32), who, in his
poverty, was forced to mind pigs before he came to his senses
and returned to his father.

13 **fear** the fear is that he might not be saved. To despair of the
possibility of one's own salvation was considered the worst
spiritual state into which one could fall.

14 **thread**   life was sometimes pictured as a thread spun out and
finally cut by the Fates; here, however, the poet spins his own life
and is, consequently, solely responsible for all his wrongdoing.
perish   it is perhaps significant that in the Authorized Version
of the Bible this word appears in the story of the prodigal son:
'and I perish with hunger! I will arise and go to my father' (St
Luke 15:17–18).
shore   which way does this image work? Is he the drowning
sailor who dies just as he reaches the shore, or is the sea a
symbol of God, which the poet fails to attain because he dies
on the shore?

16 **shine... shines**   Donne may be thinking of the words of Jesus:
'he [God] maketh his sun to rise on the evil and on the good'
(St Matthew 5:45).

17 **thou hast done**   if the pun works, this is its triumphant
resolution: the work of Christ is completed and Donne's
salvation is secured because God takes him as his own.